I0491861

Thank you for your recent purchase. We hope you love it! If you do, would you consider posting an online review? This helps us to continue providing great products and helps potential buyers to make confident decisions. Thank you in advance for your review and for being a preferred customer.

This Book Belongs To

All Illustrations Are Hand Drawn

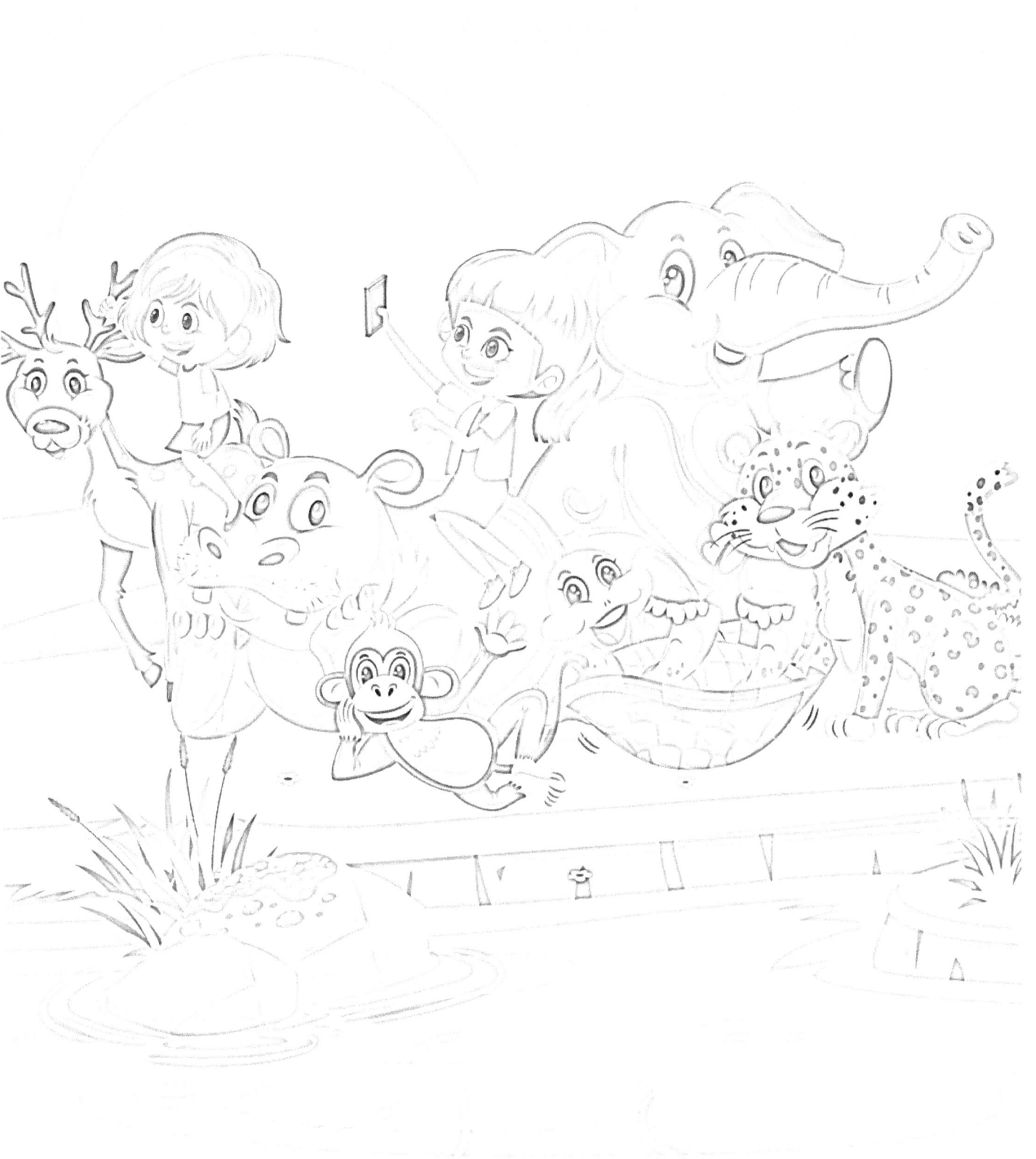

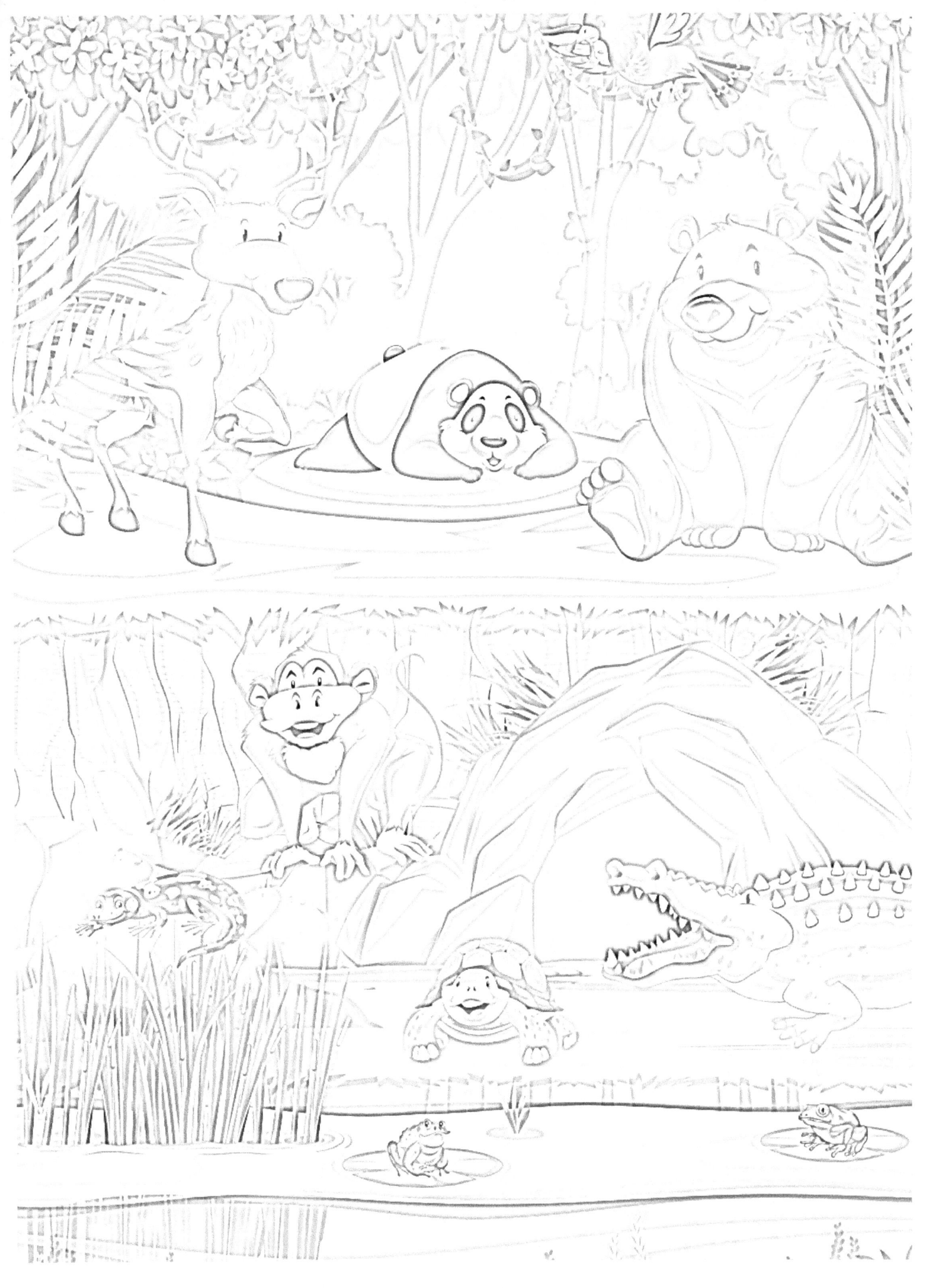

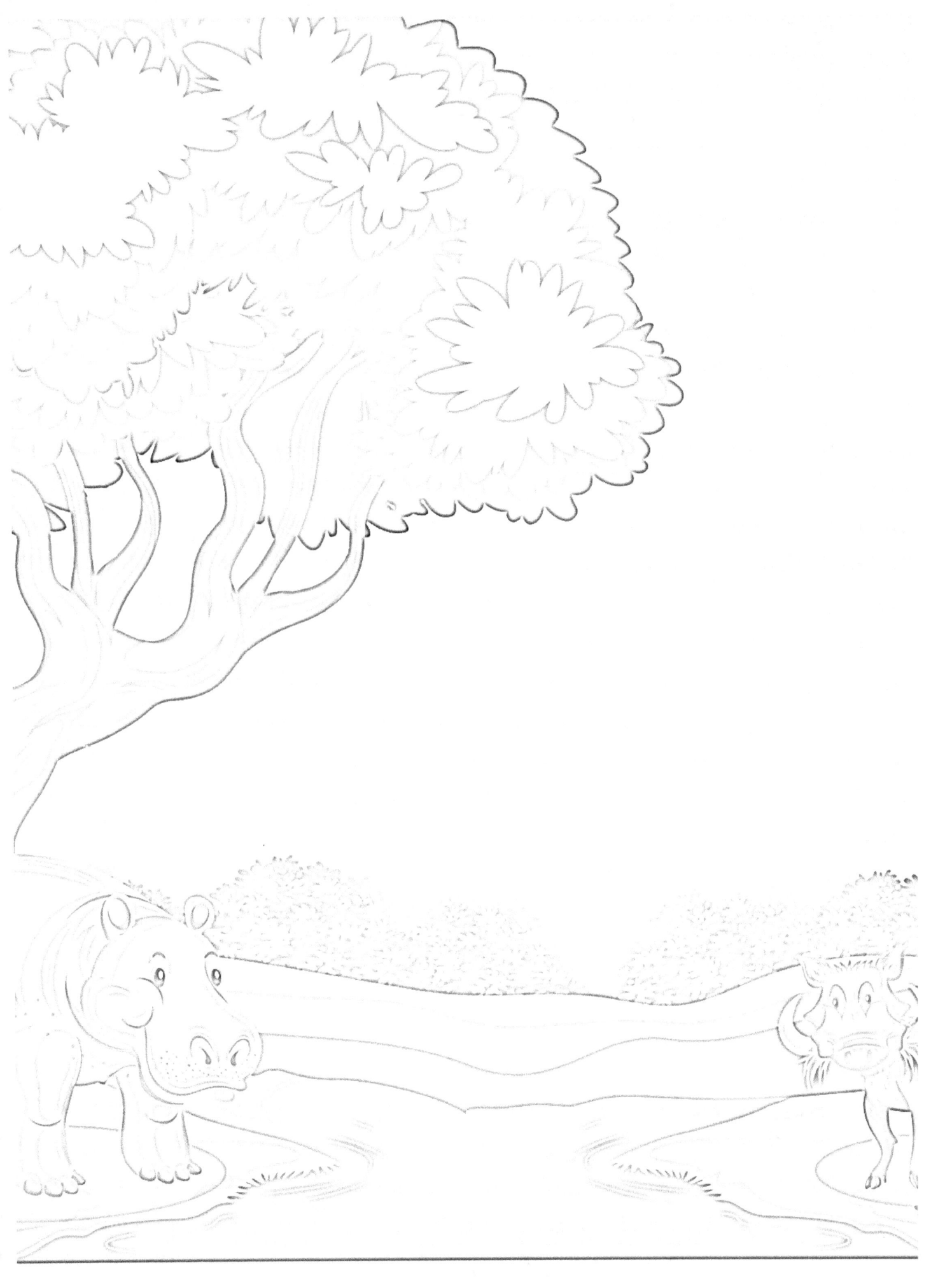

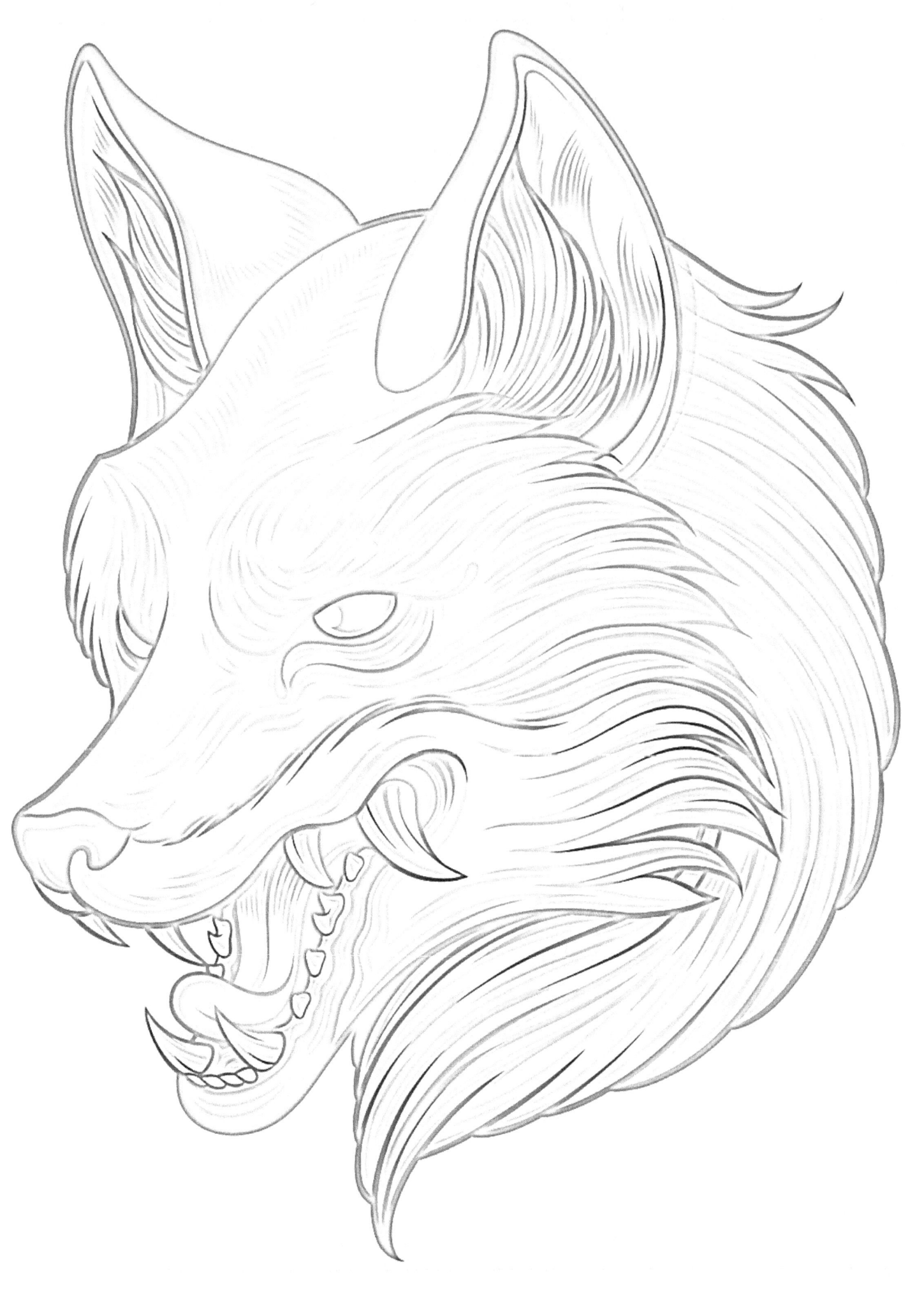

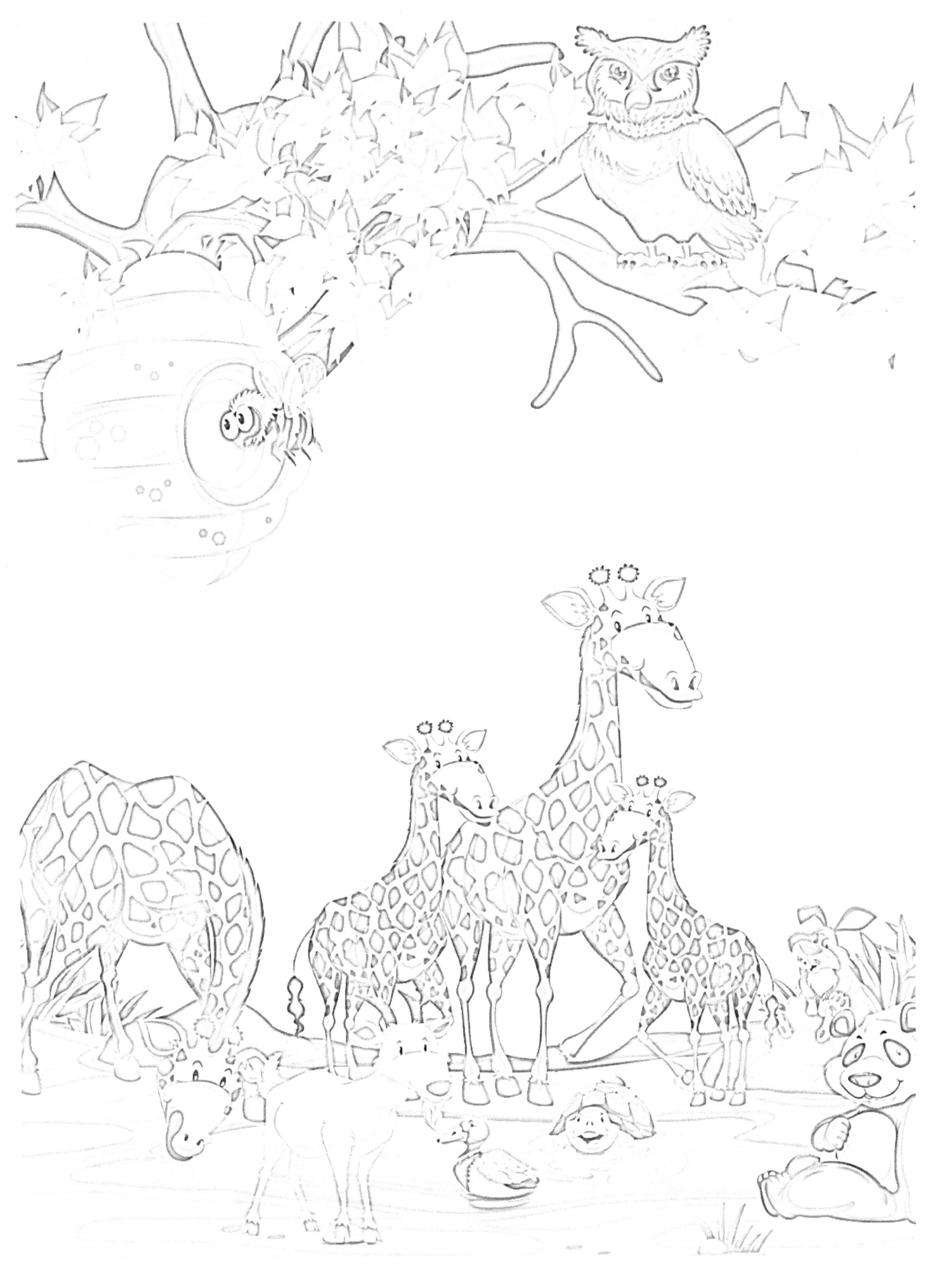

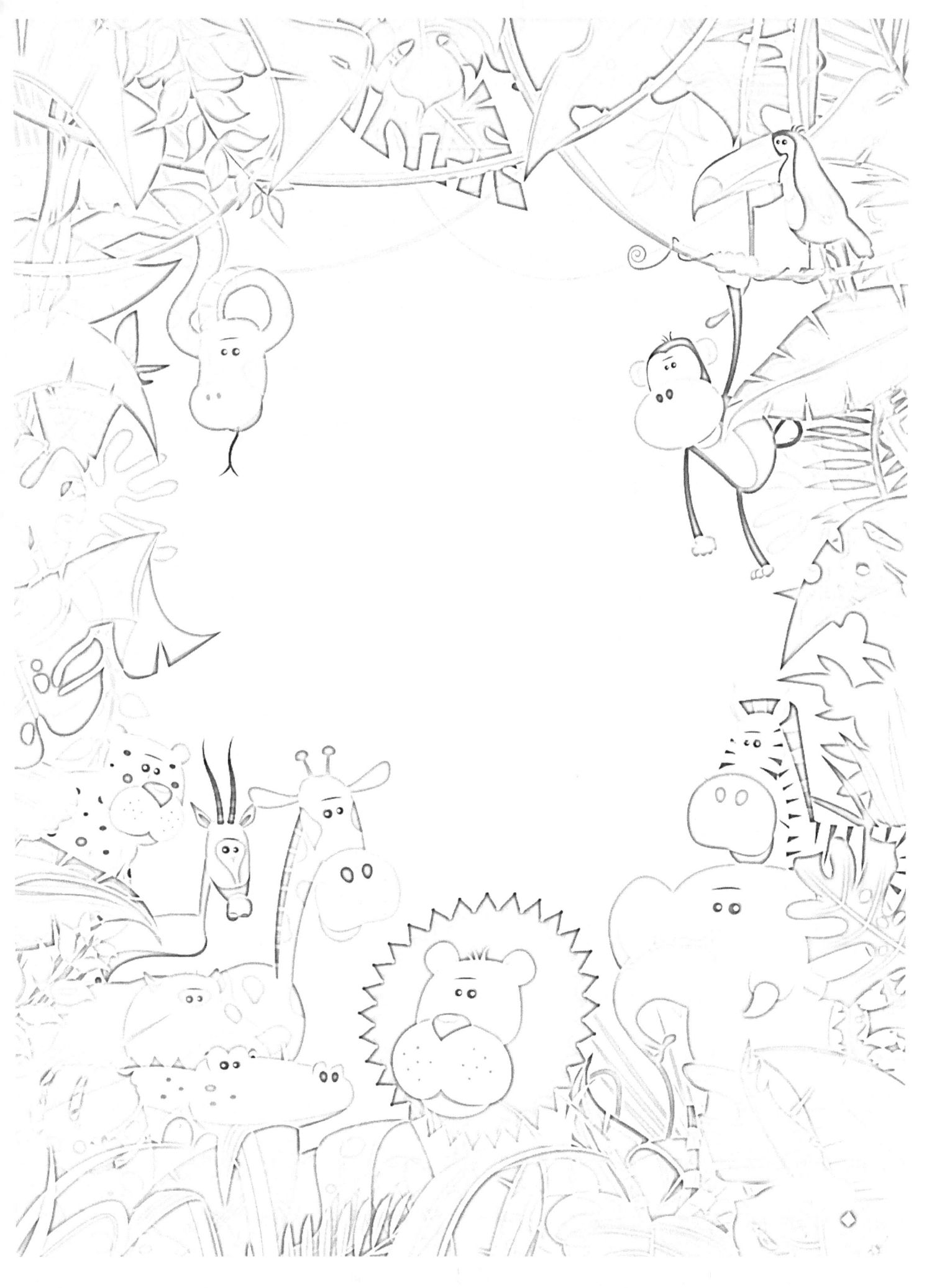

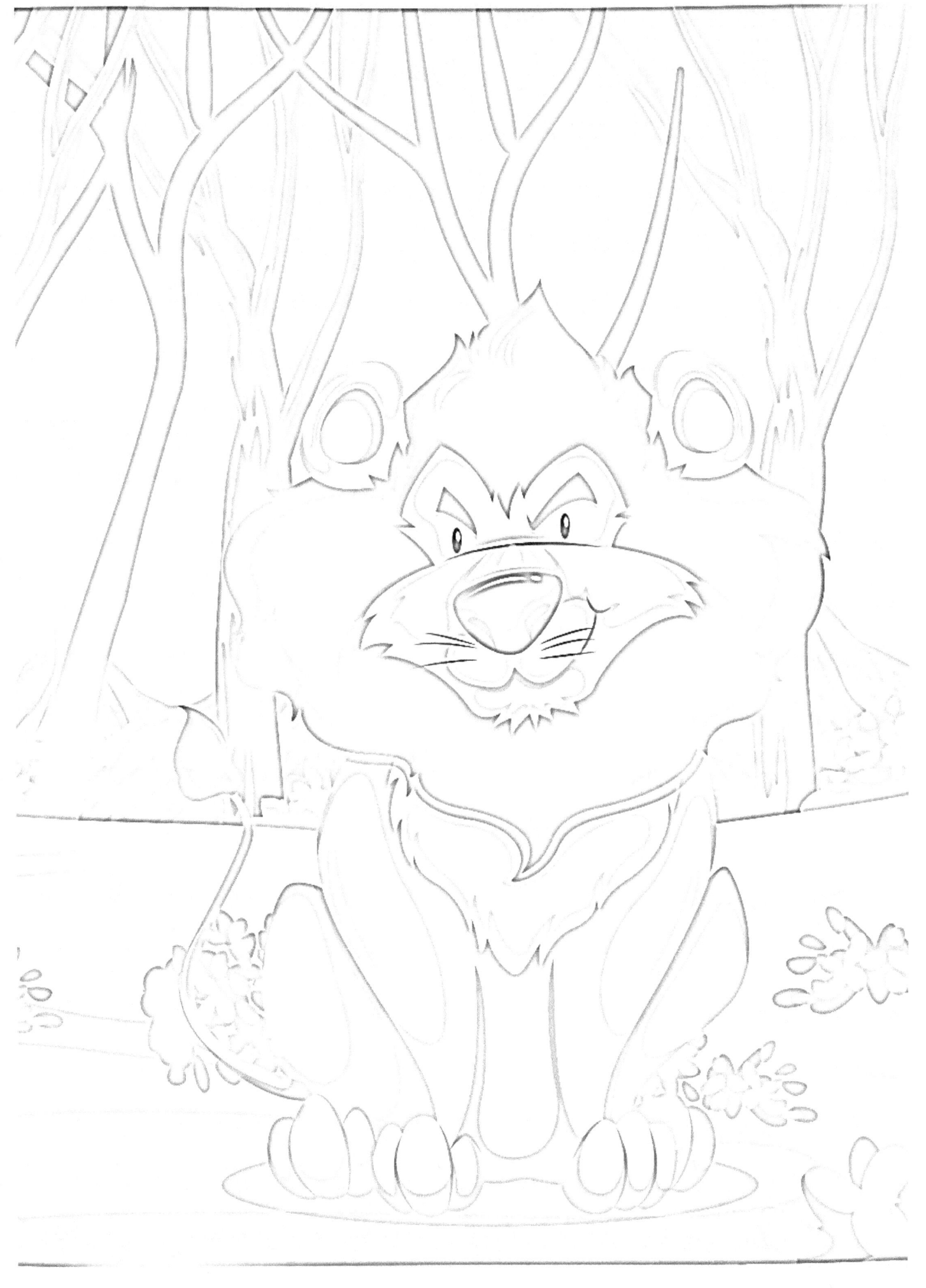

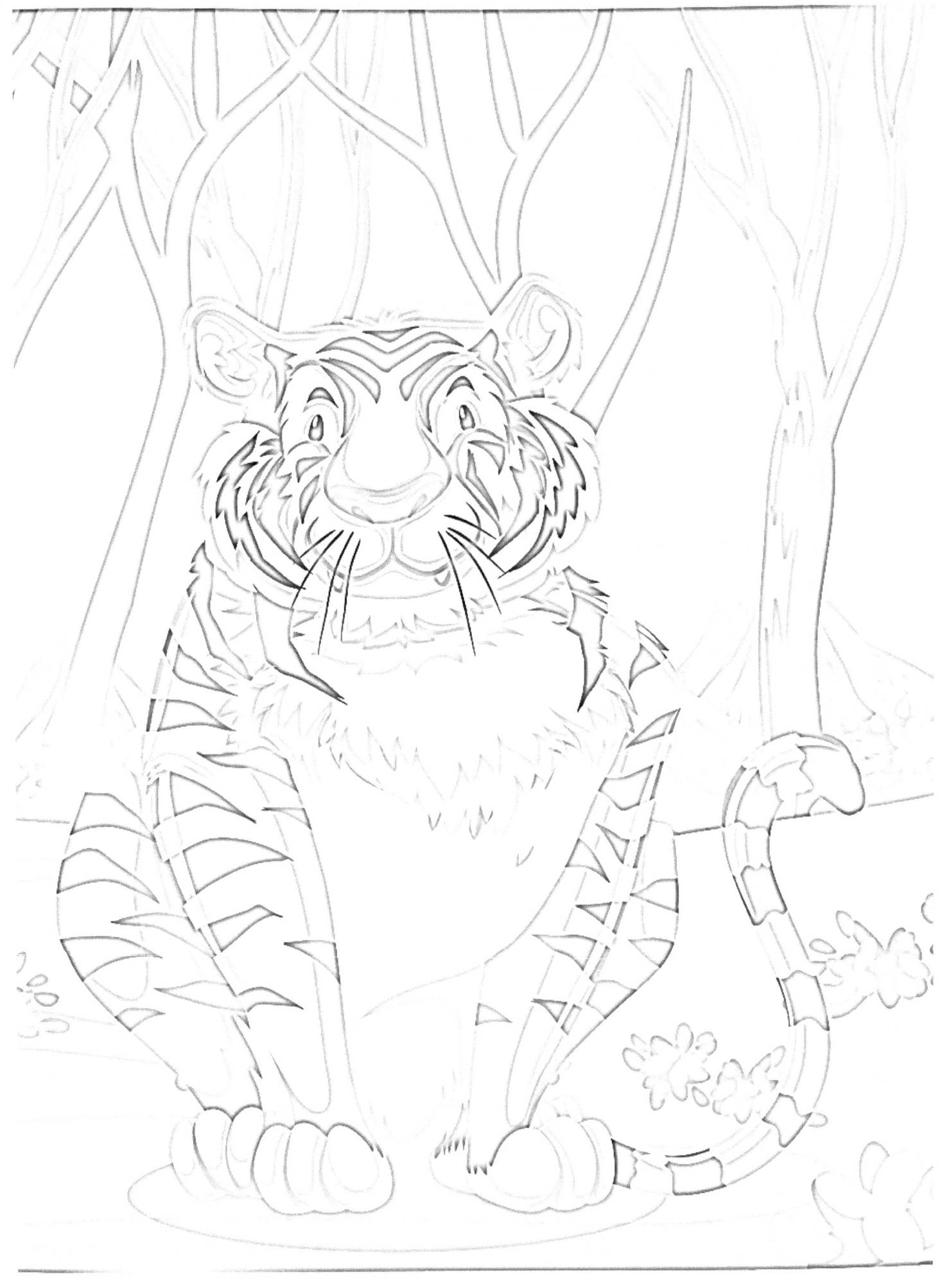

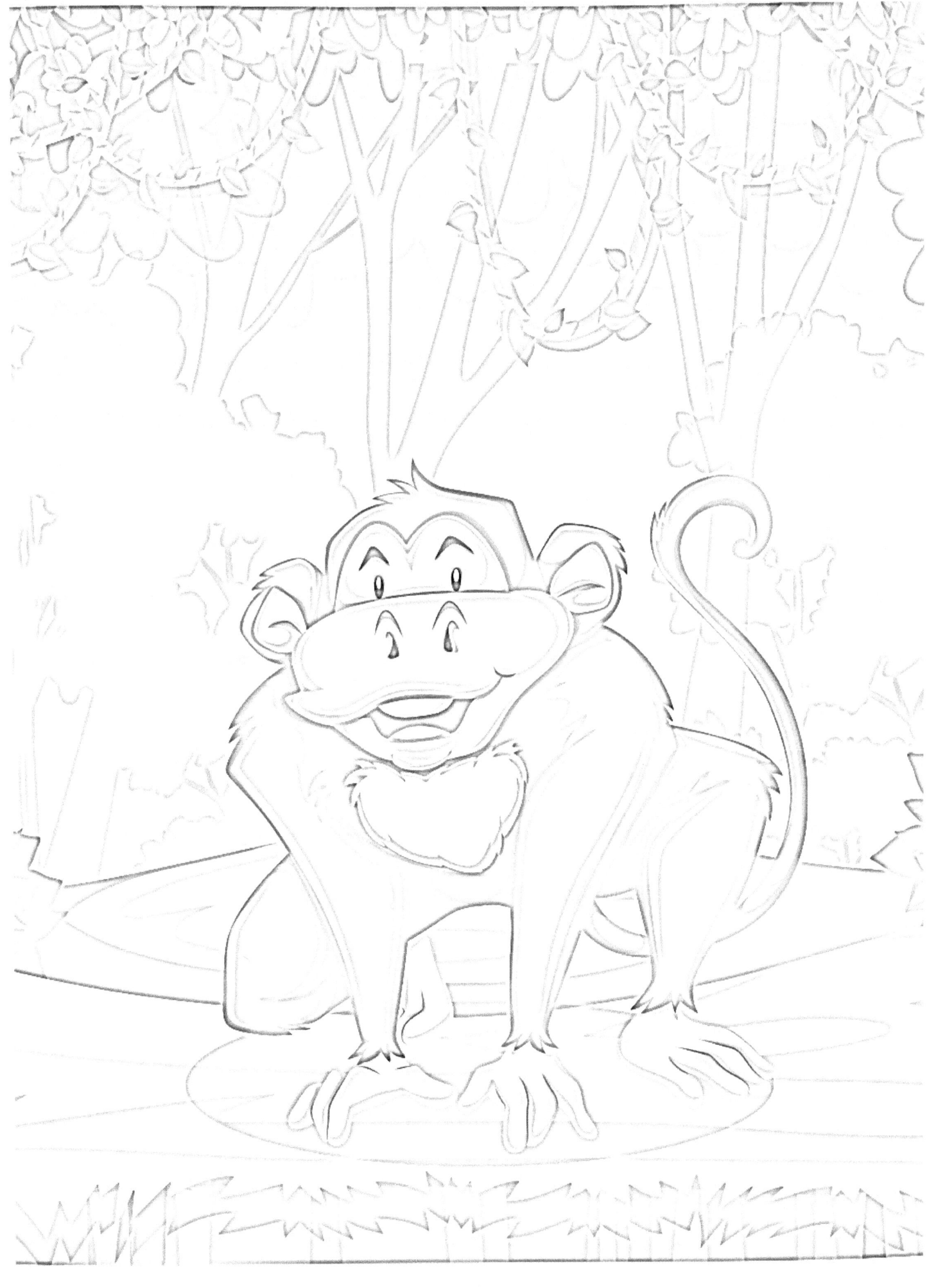

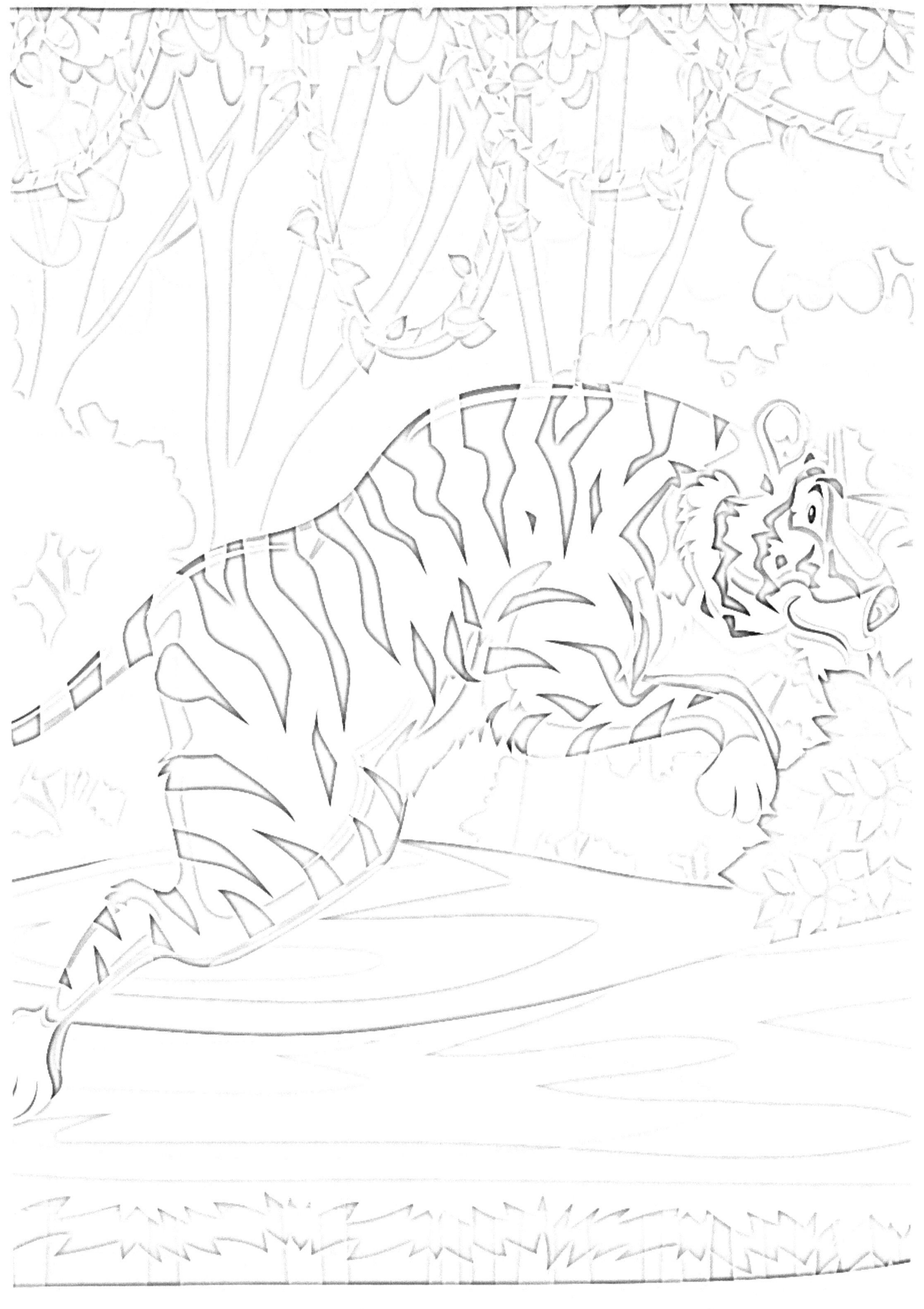

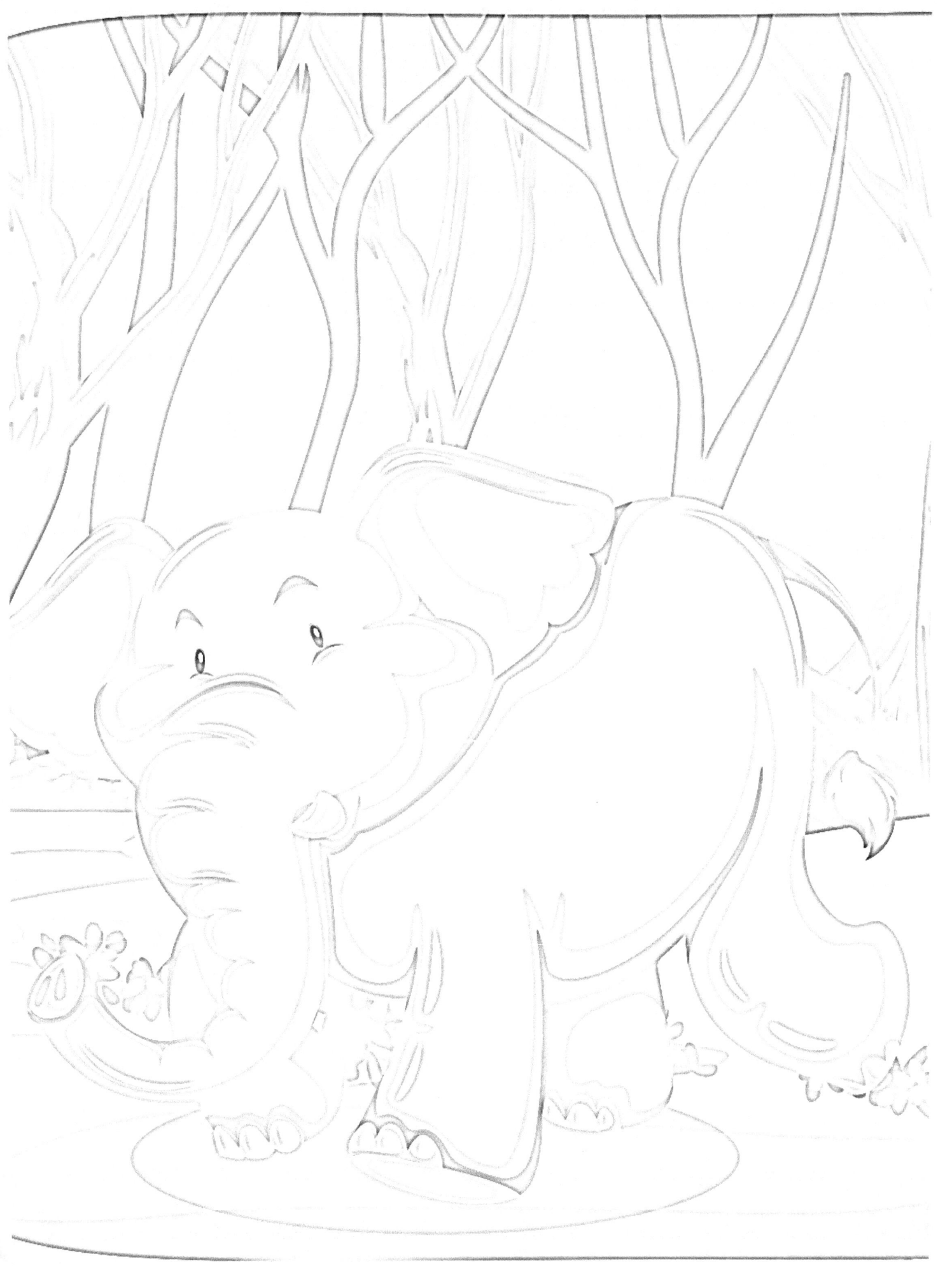

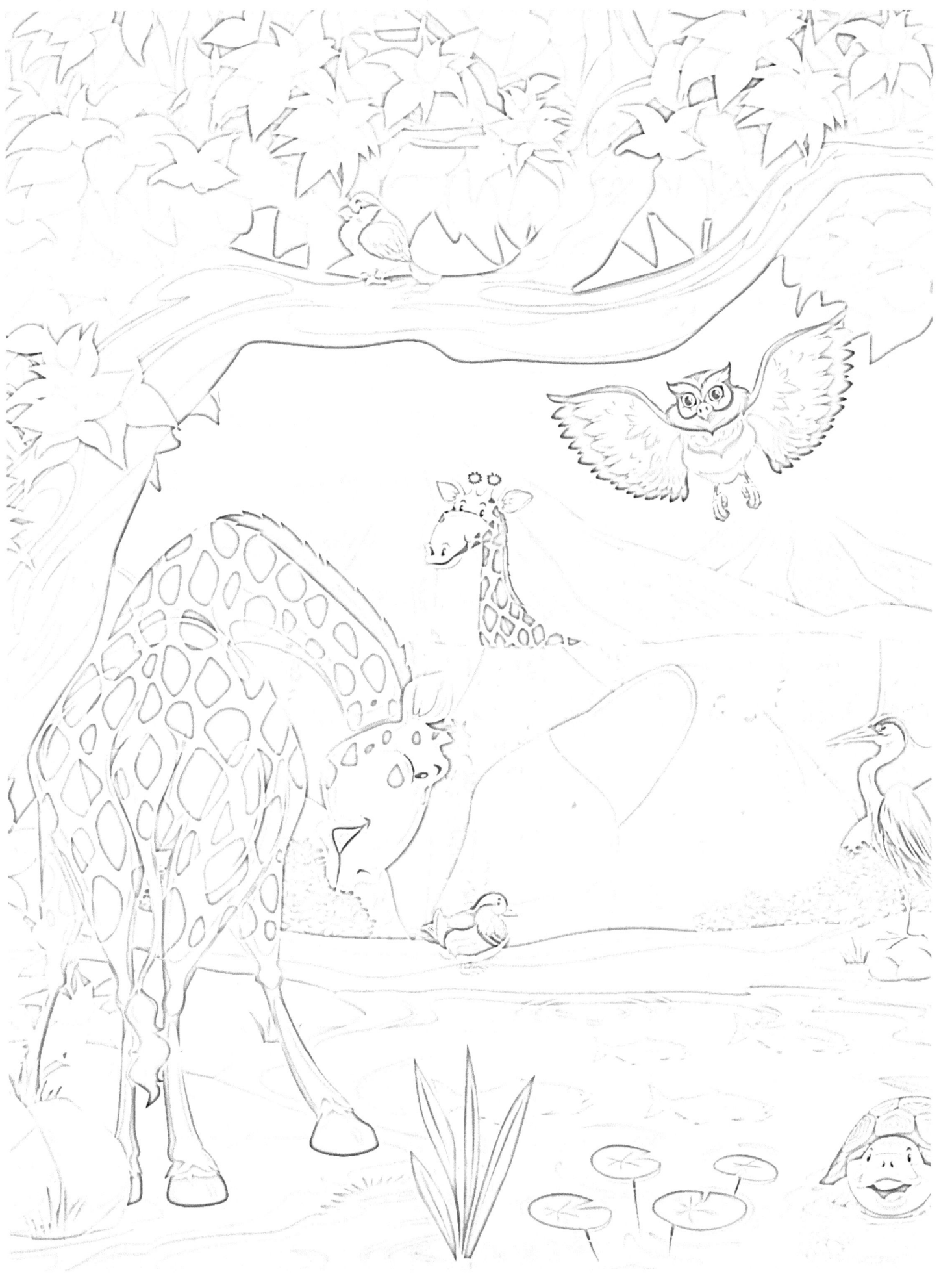

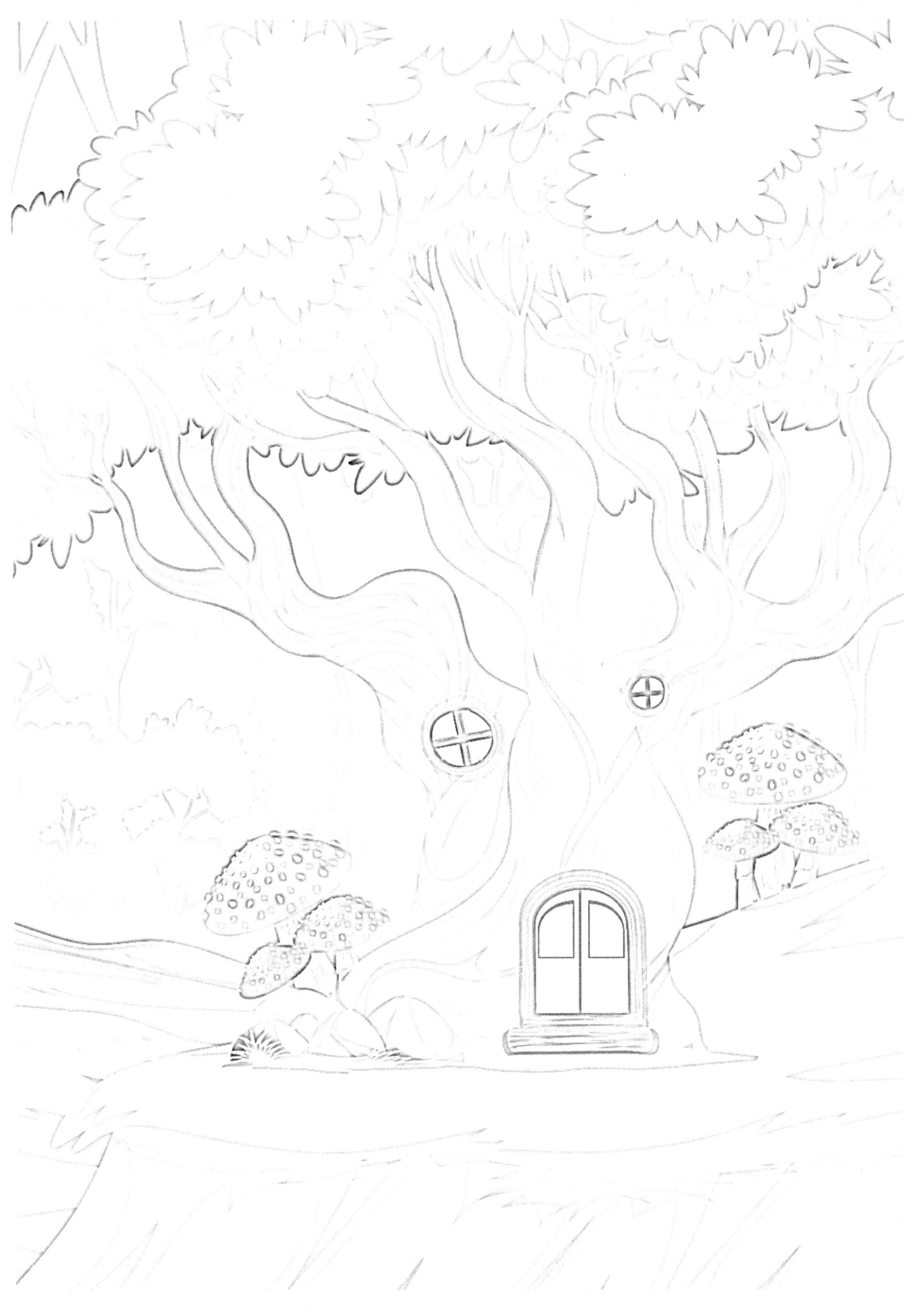

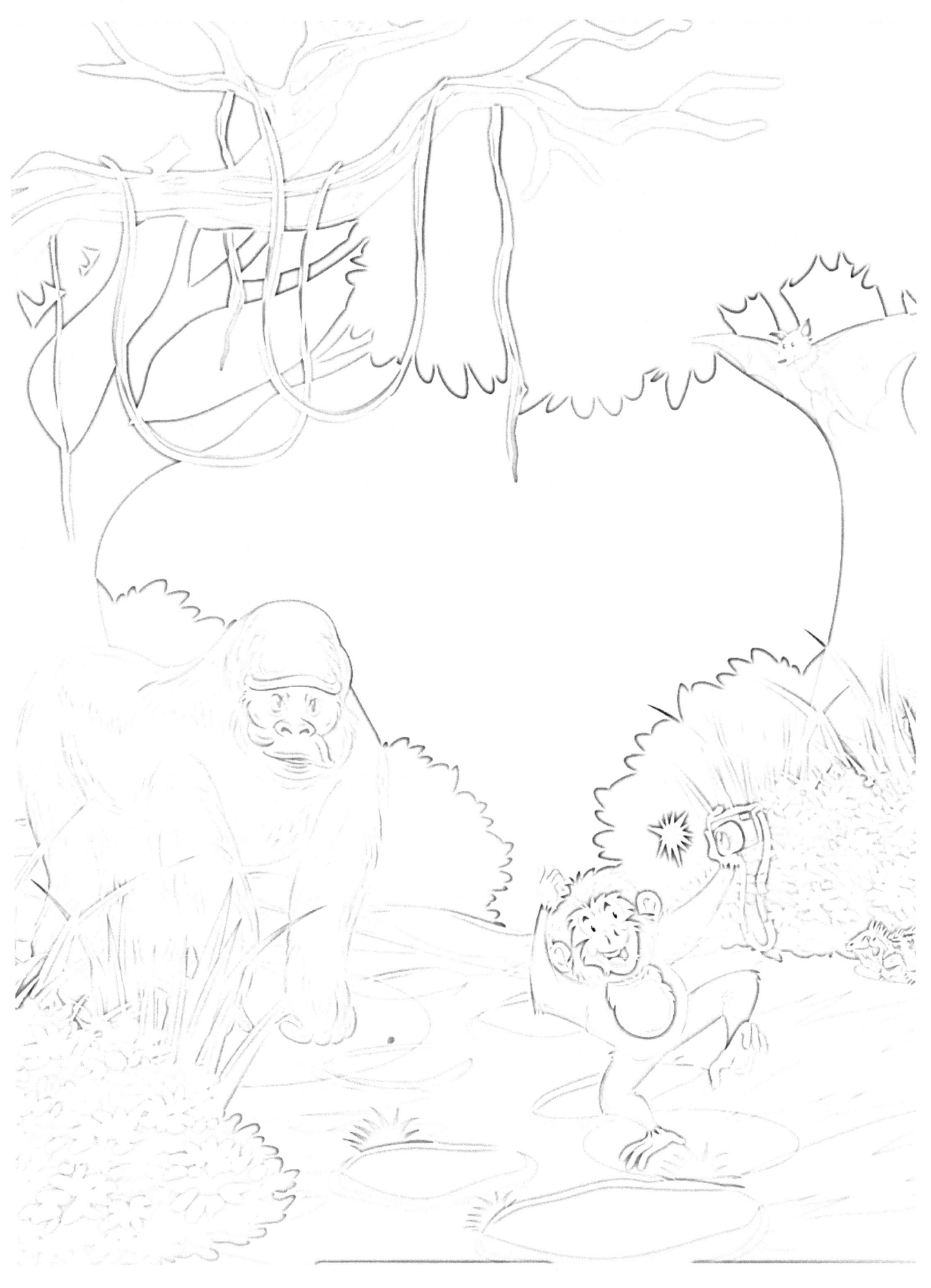

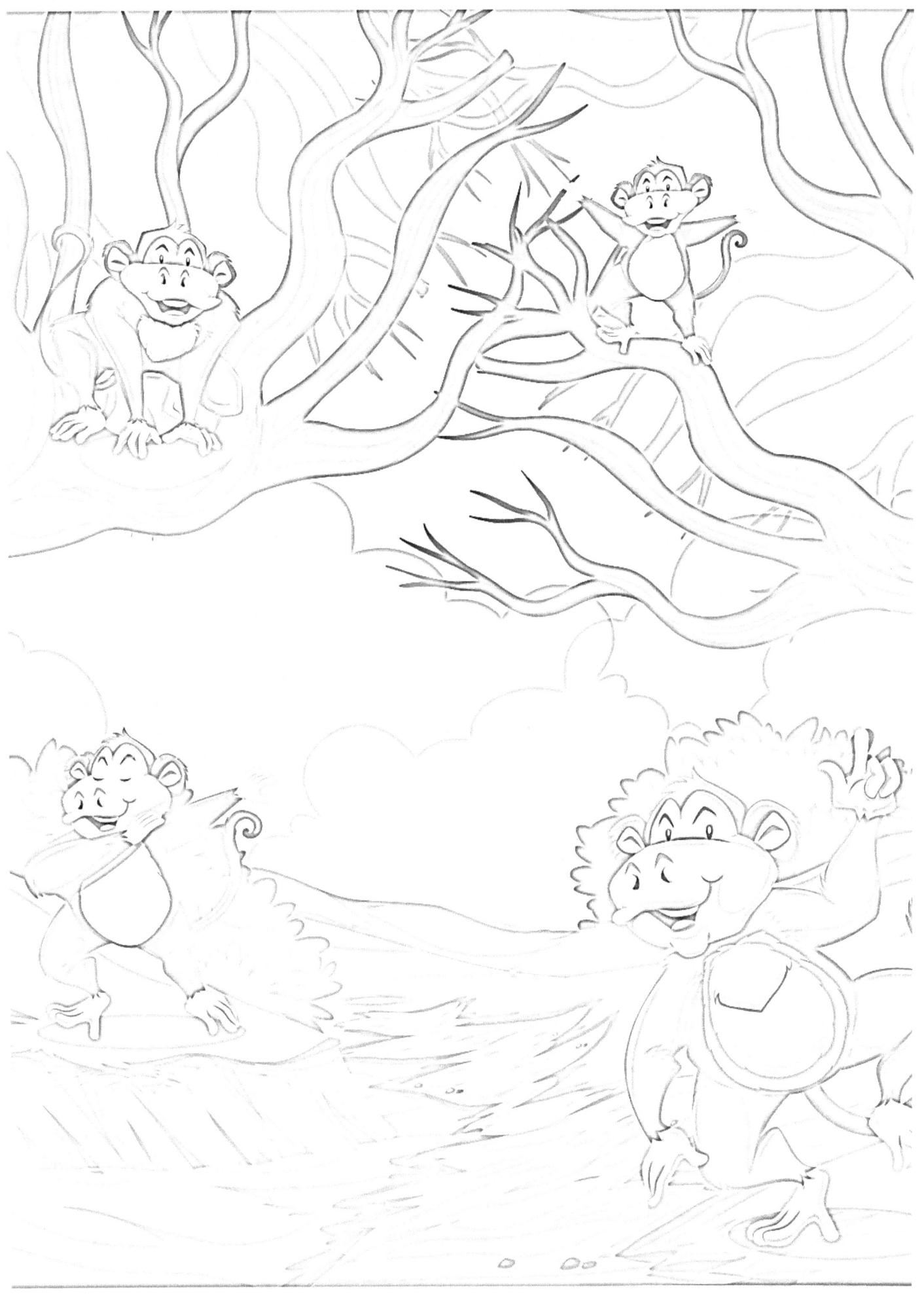

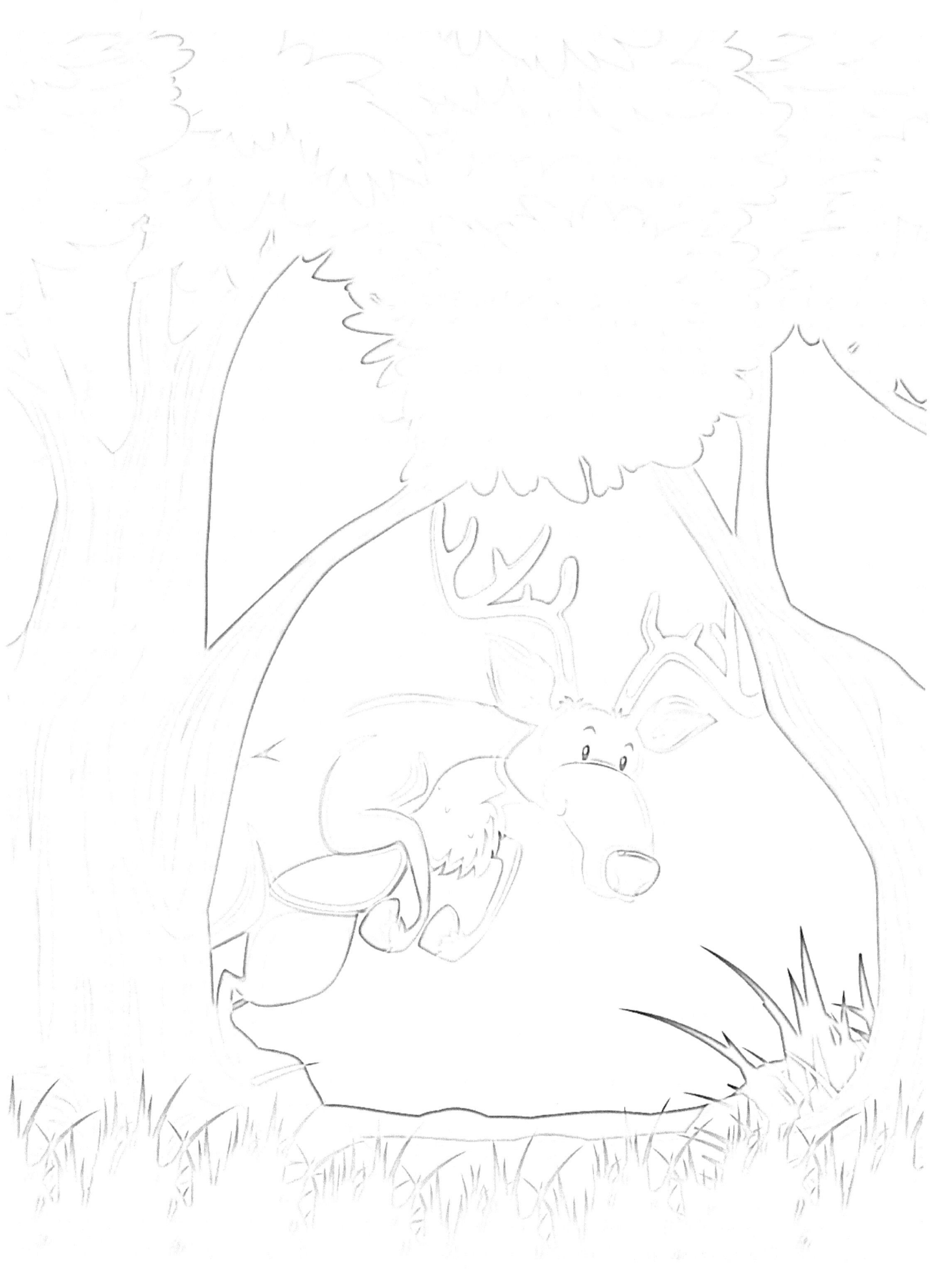

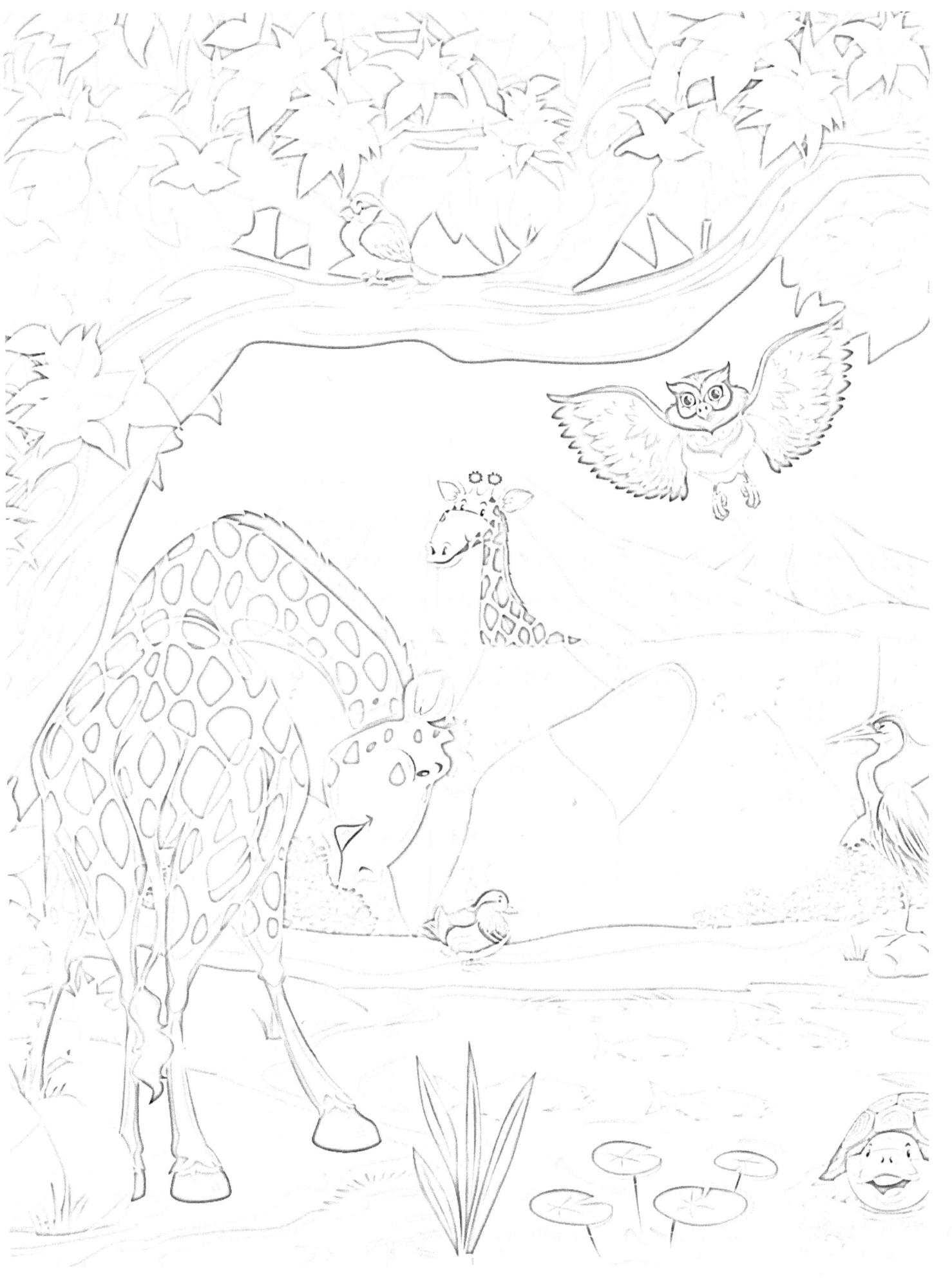

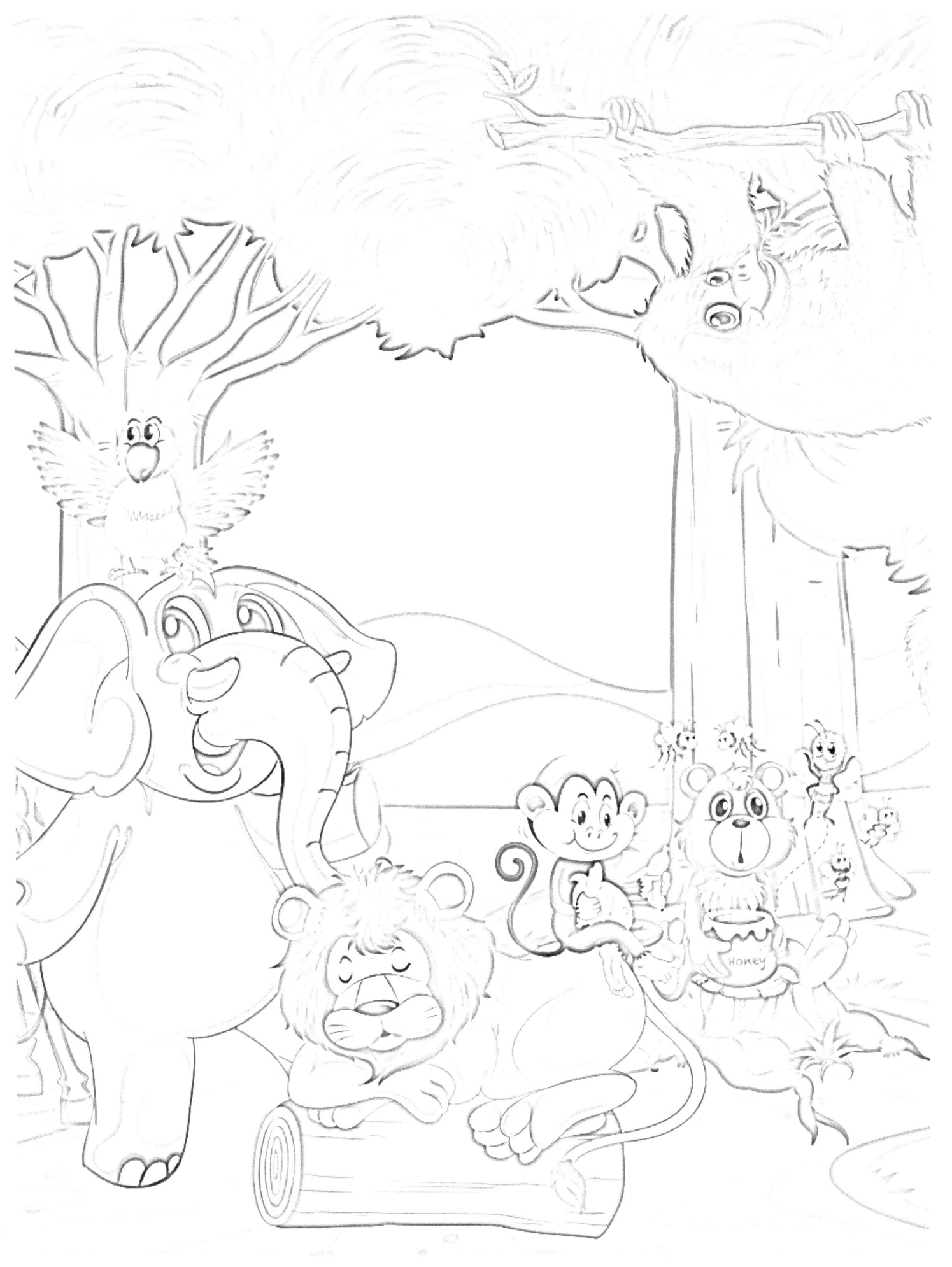

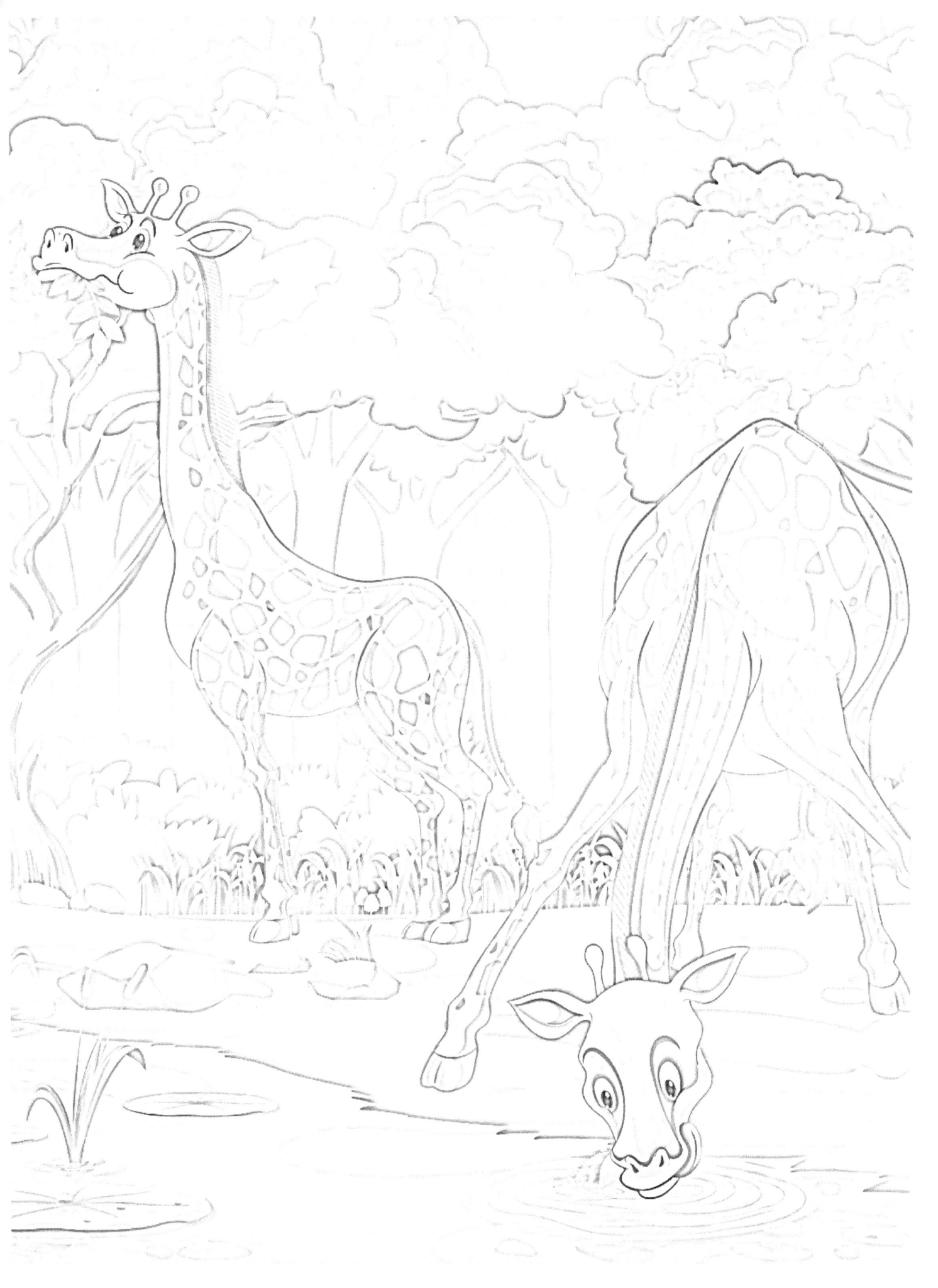

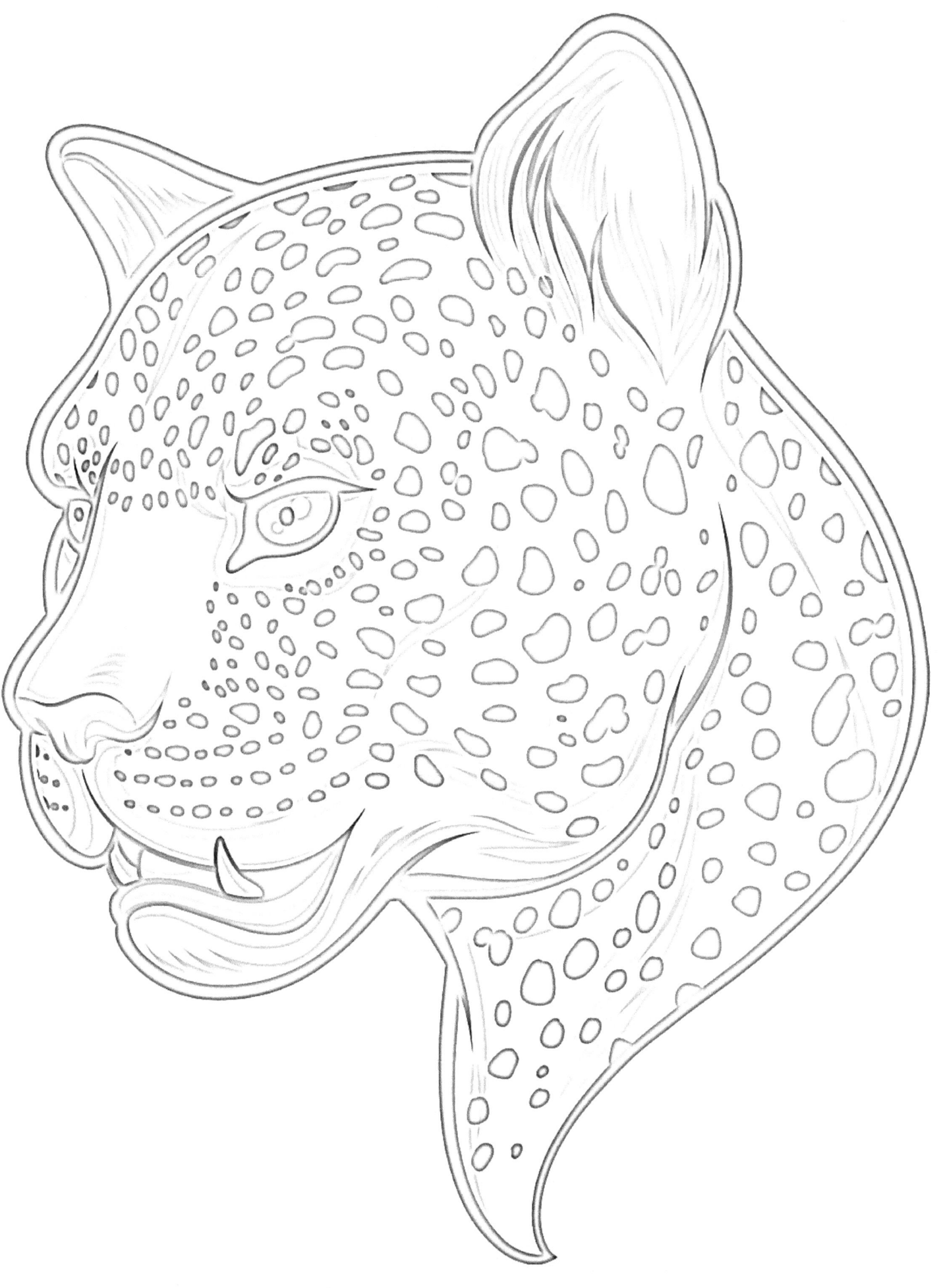

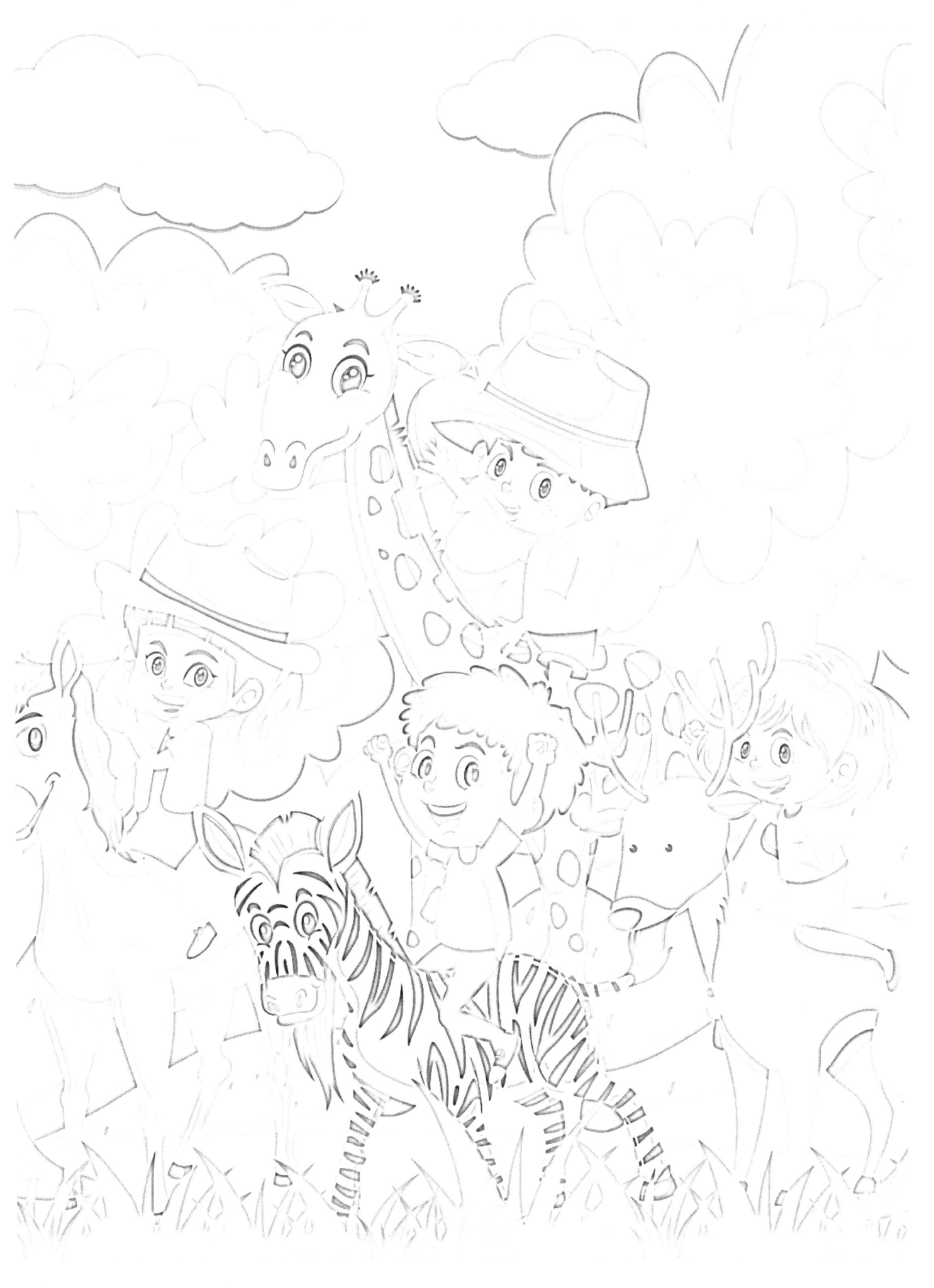

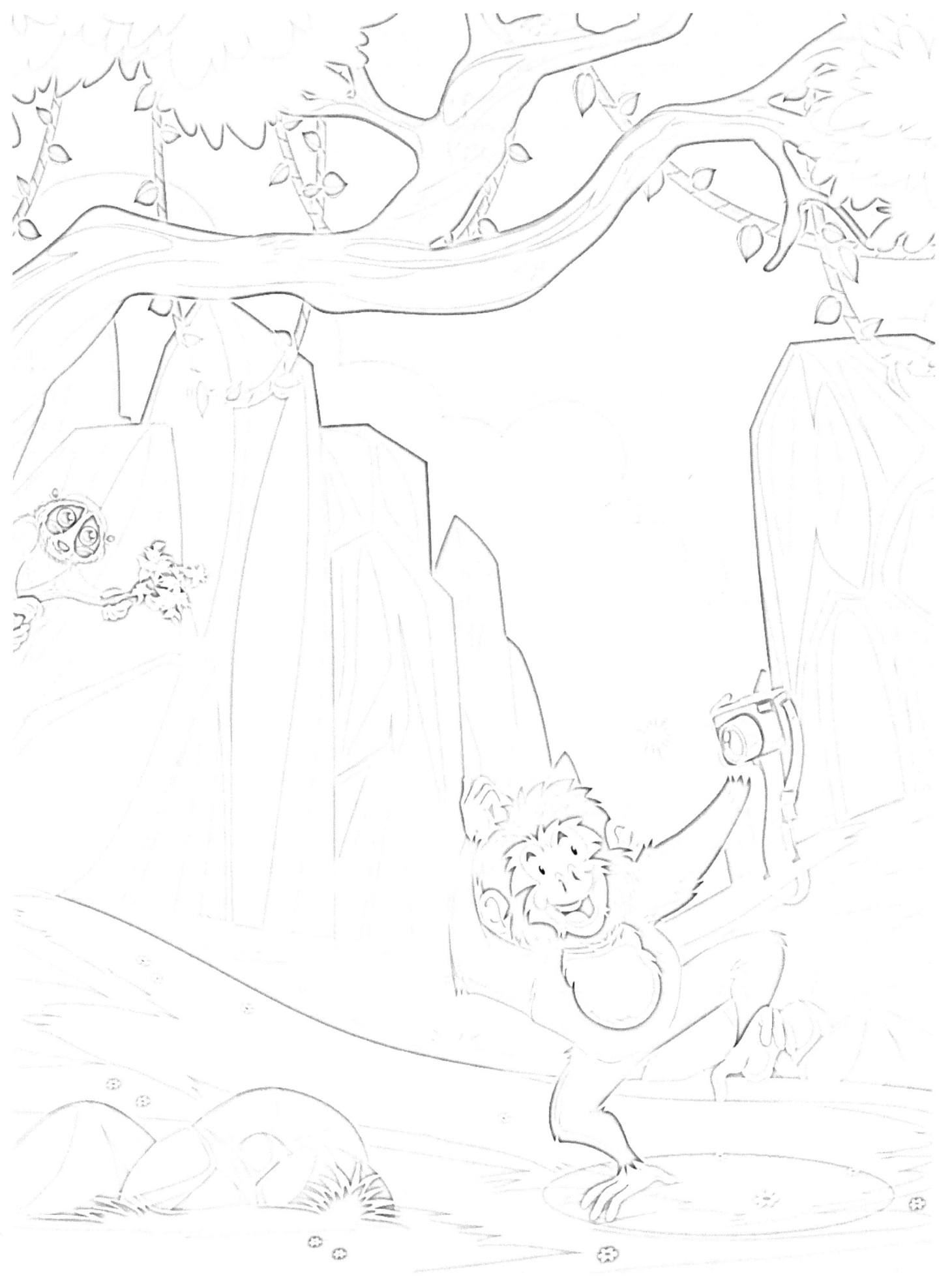

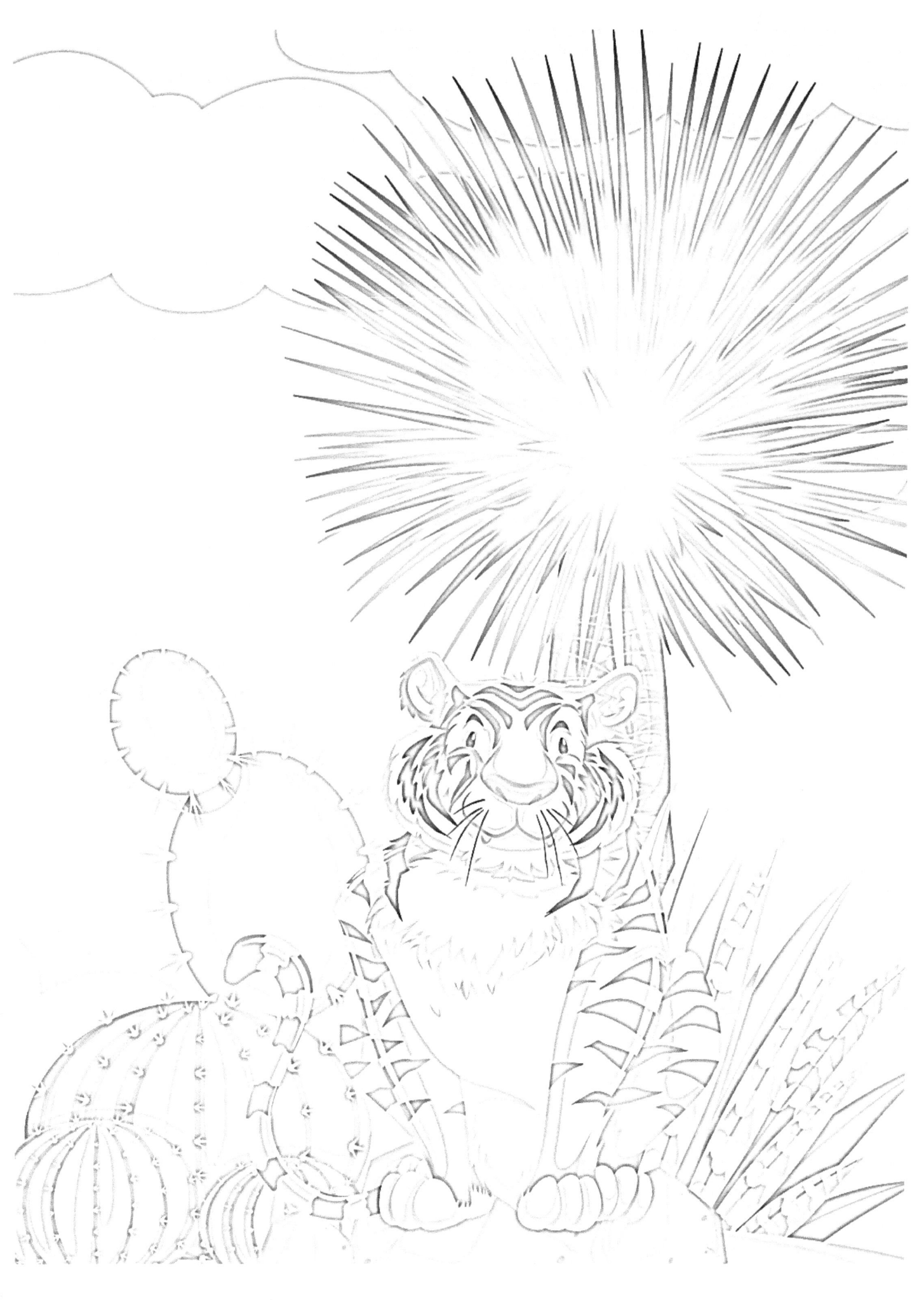

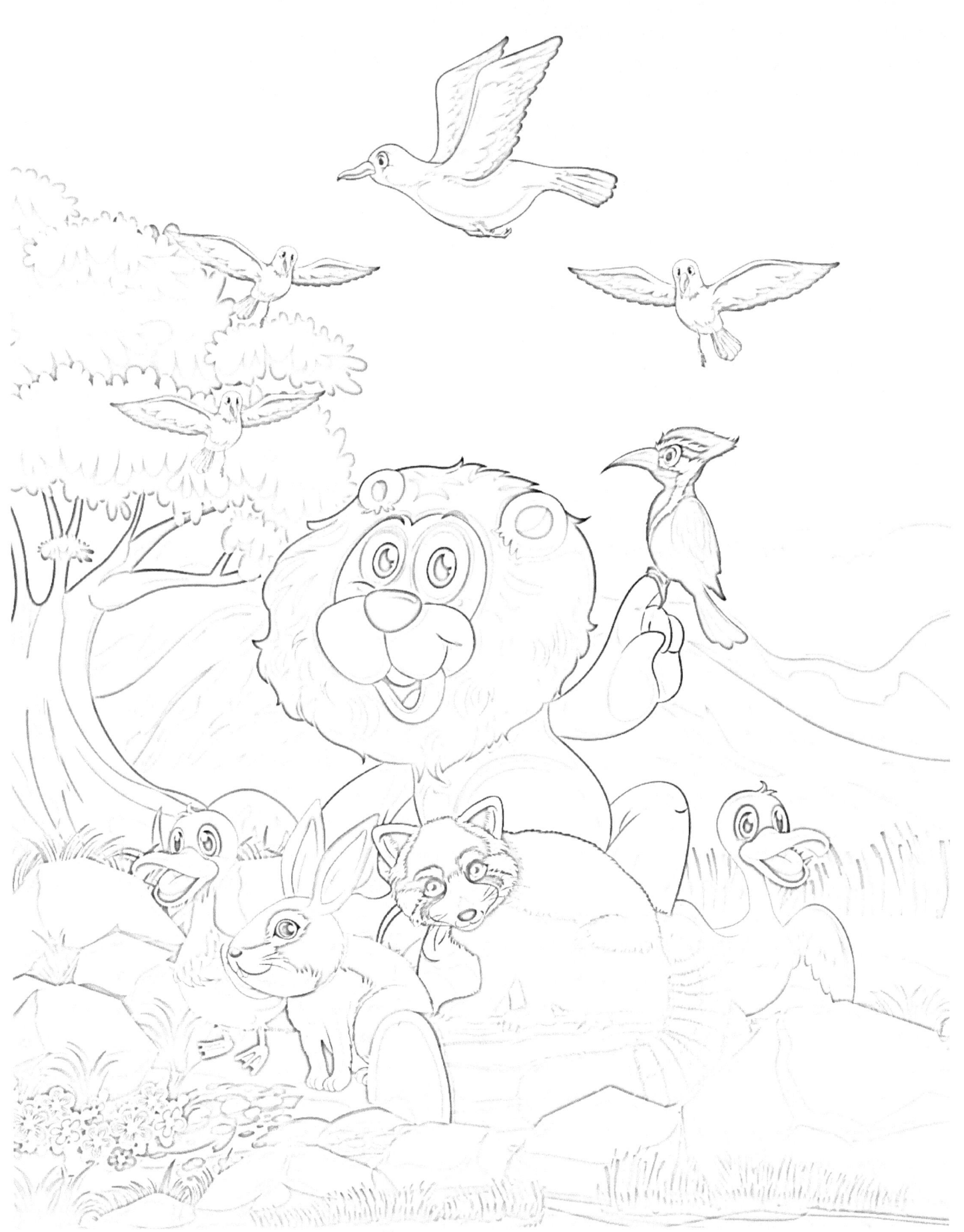

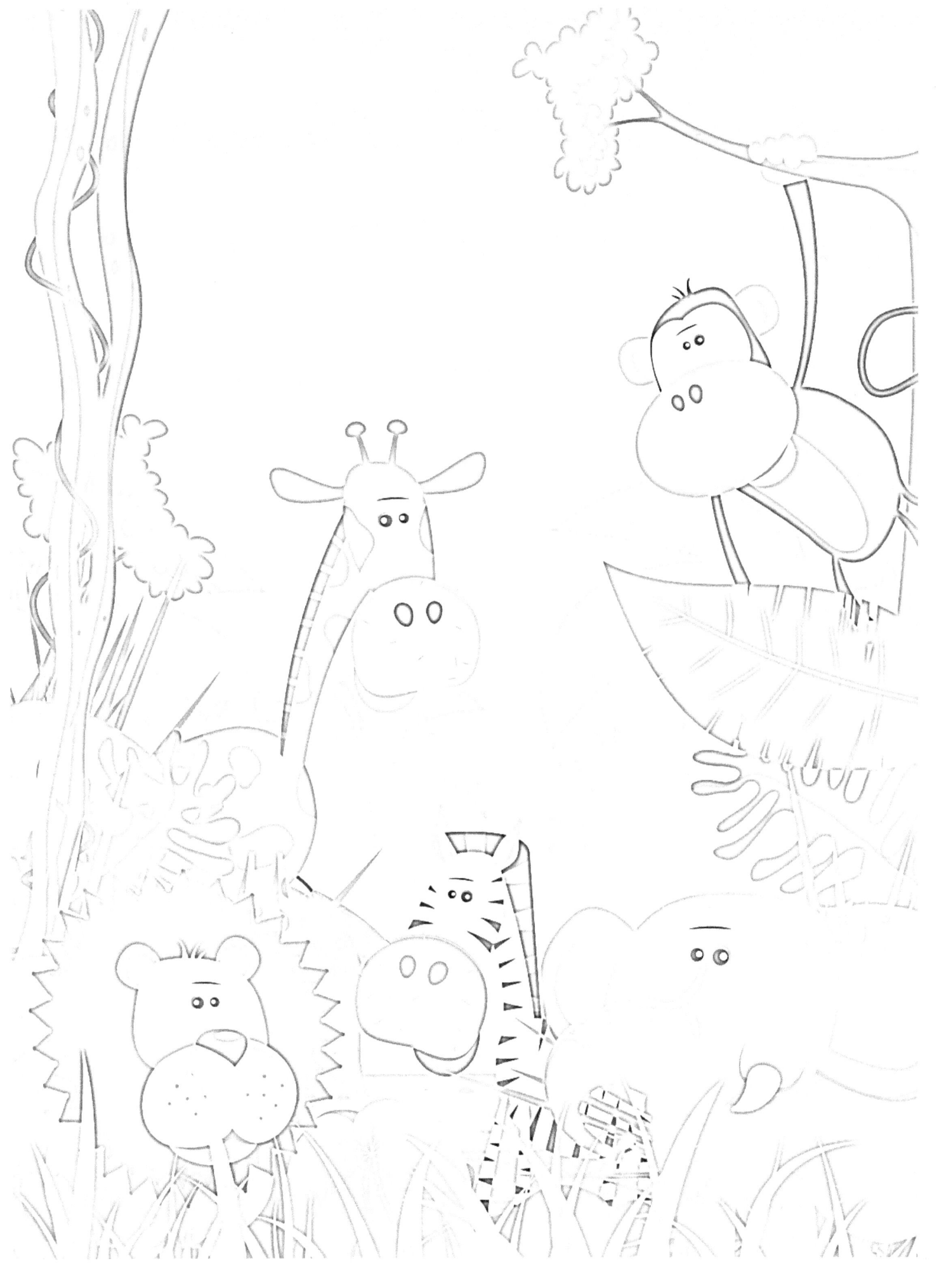

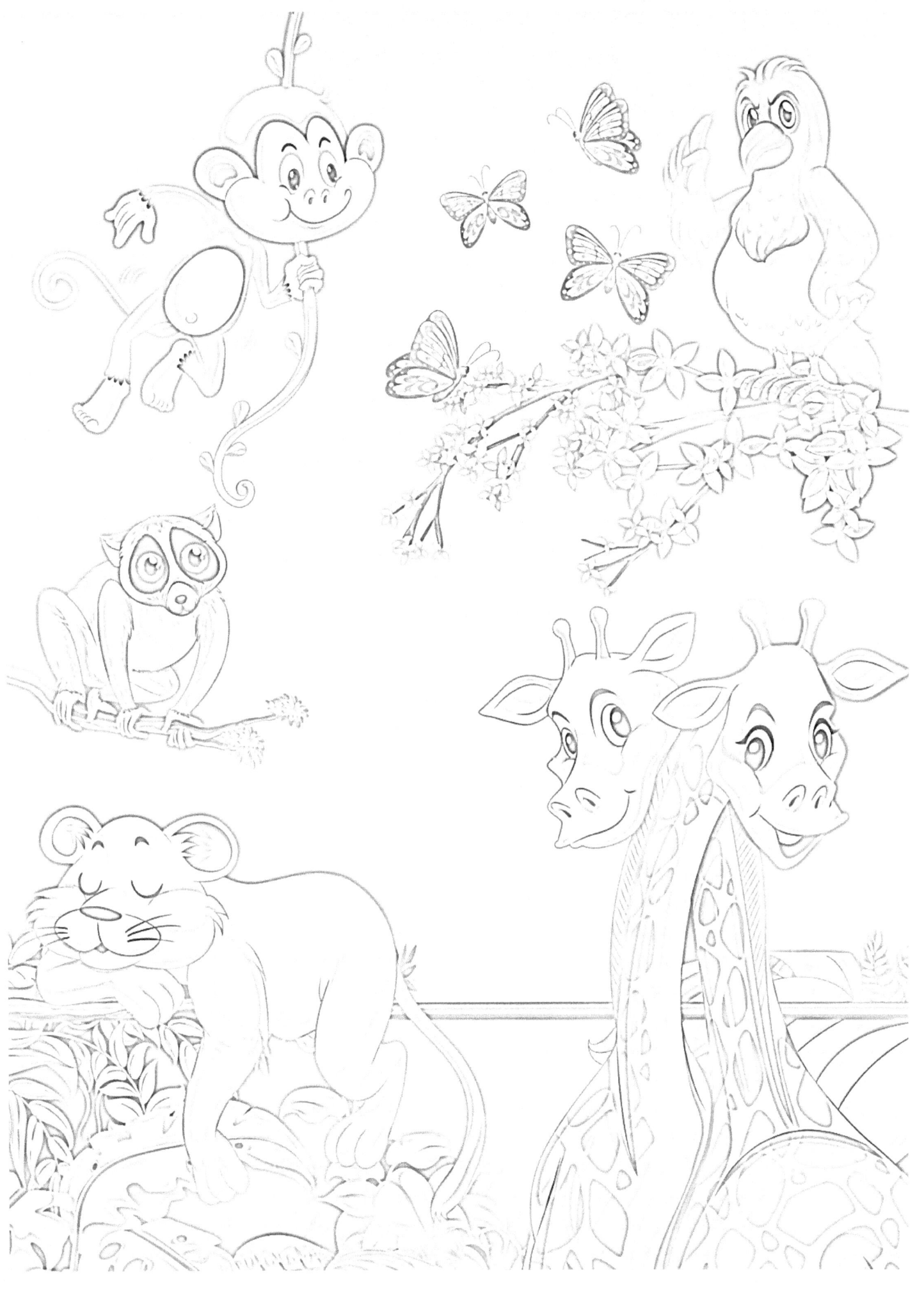

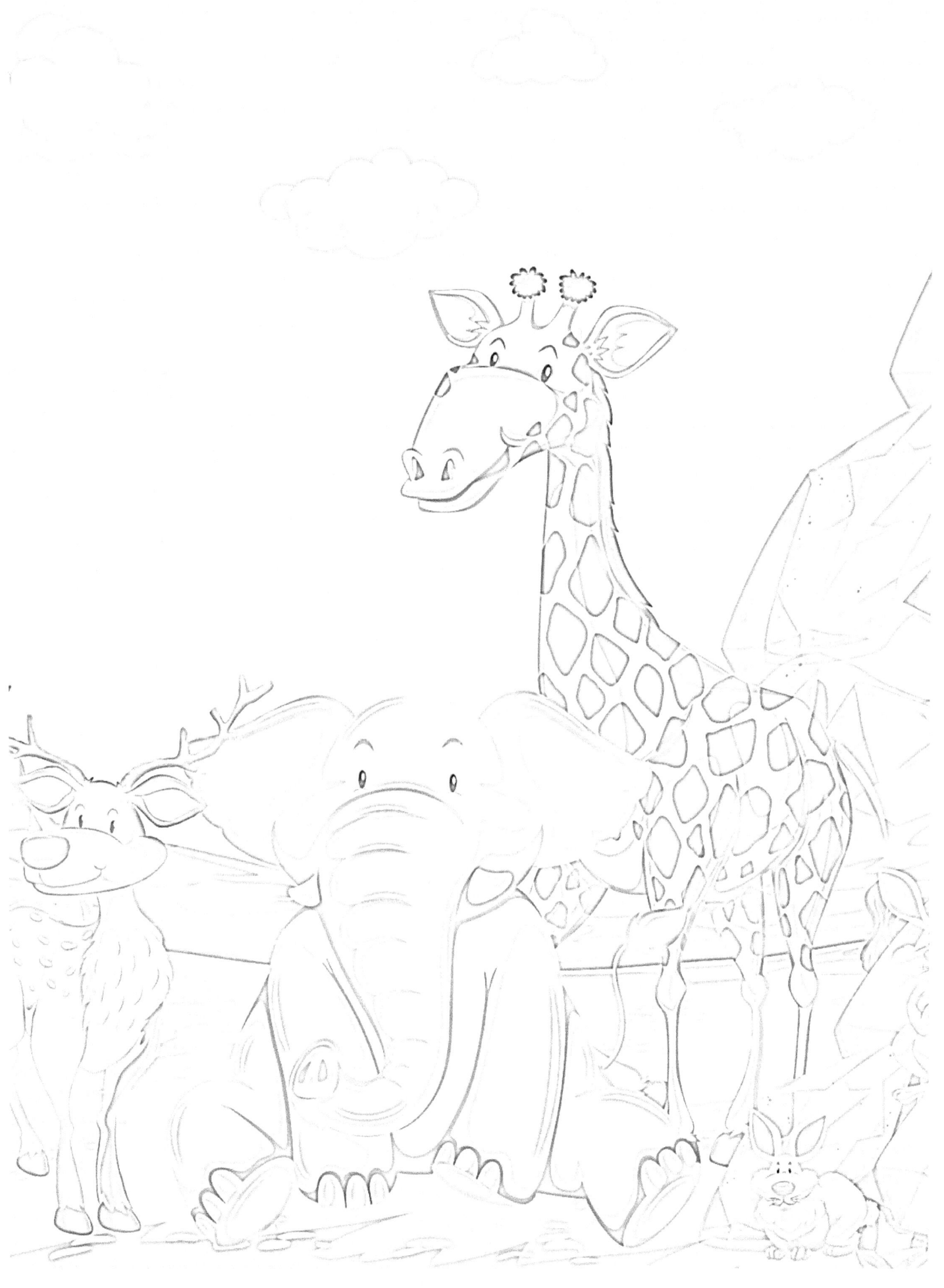

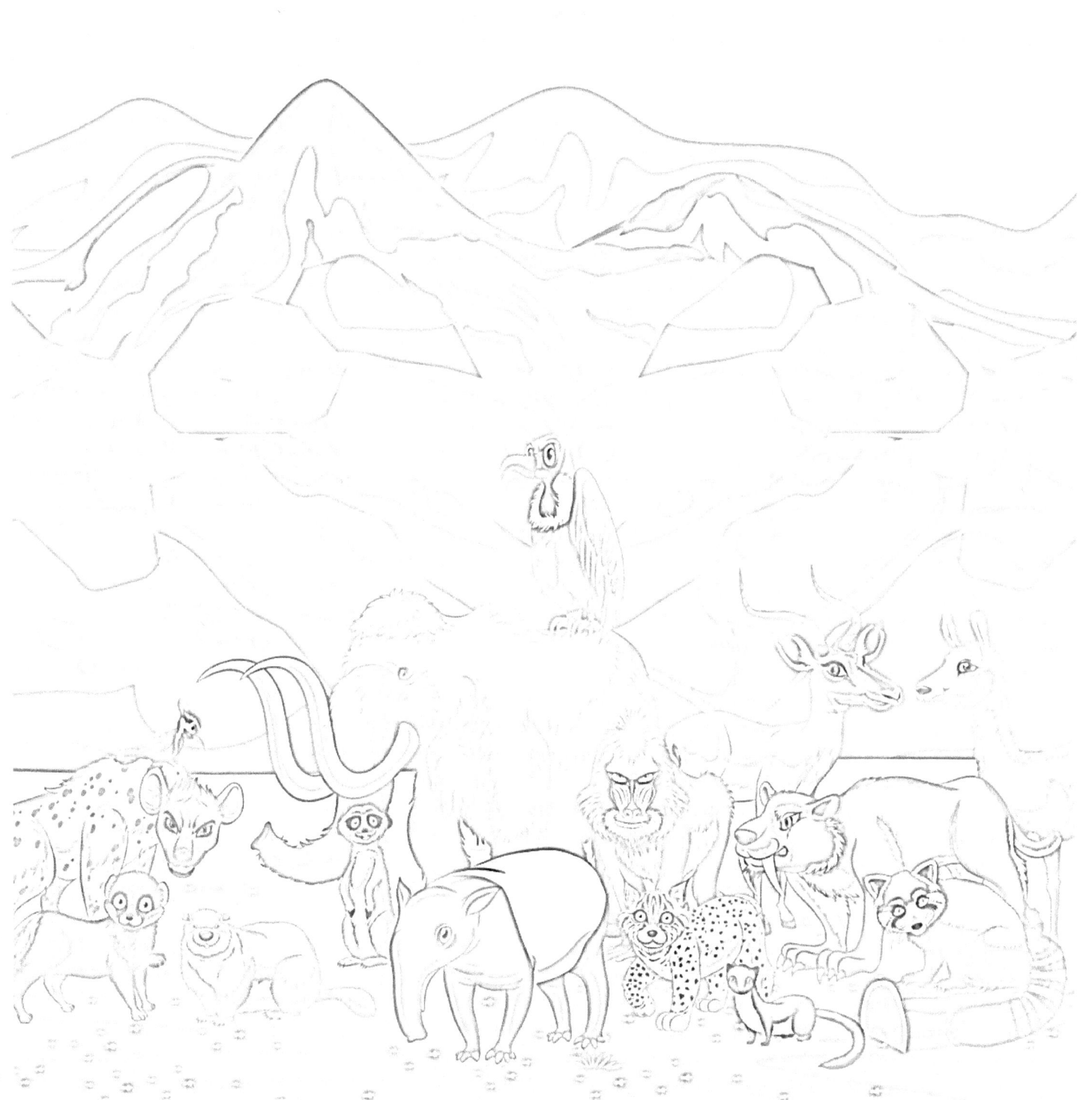

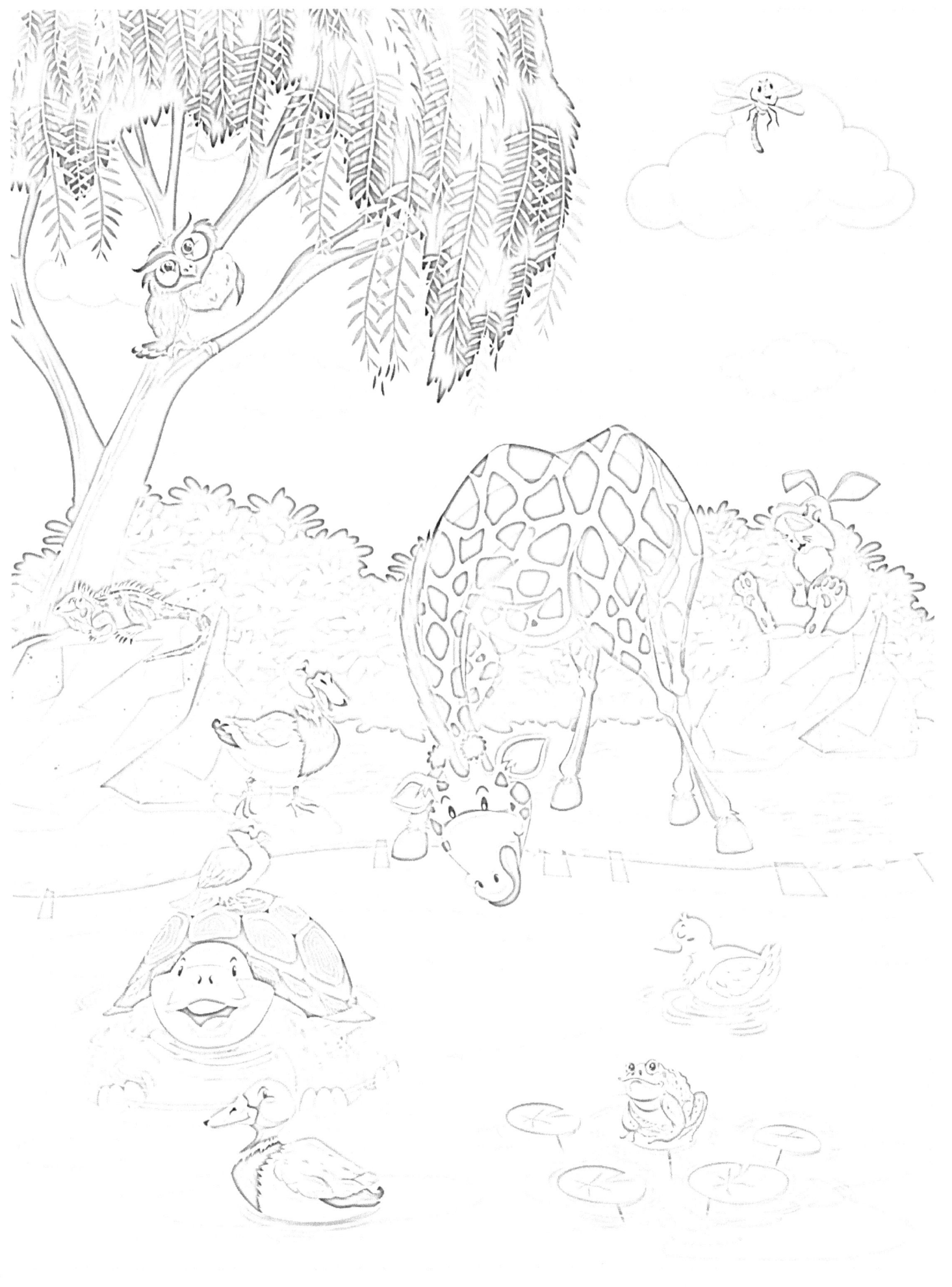

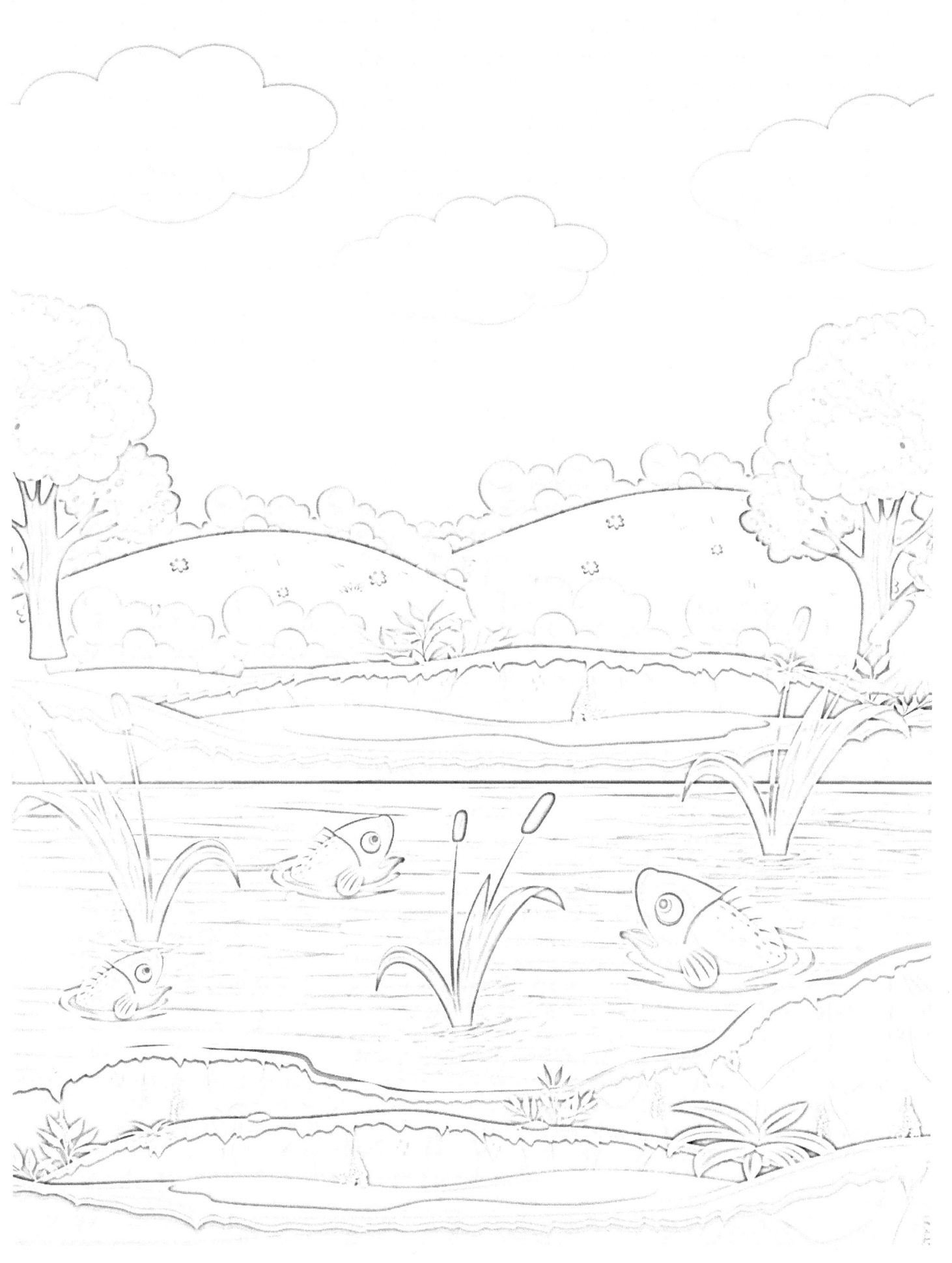

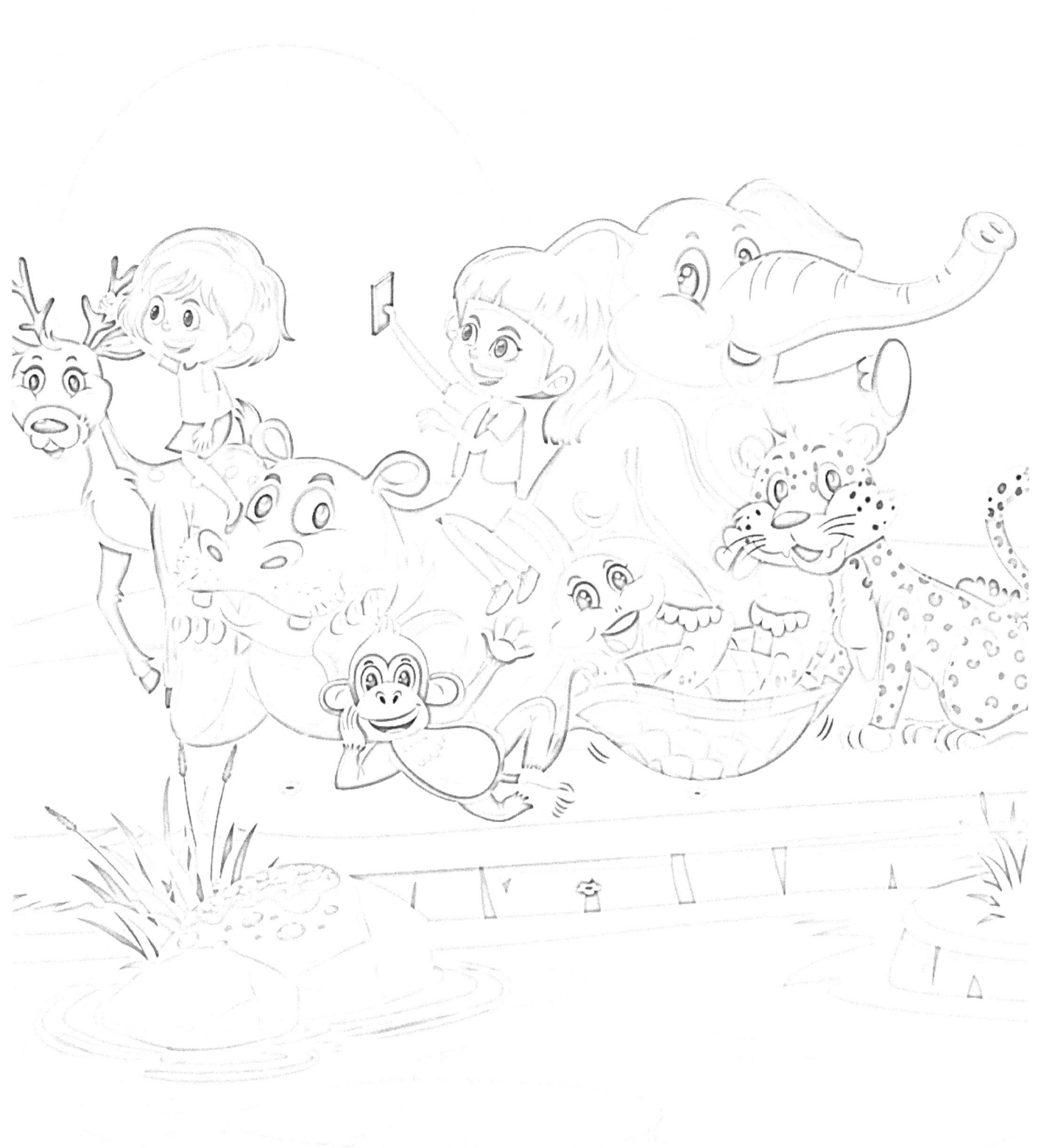

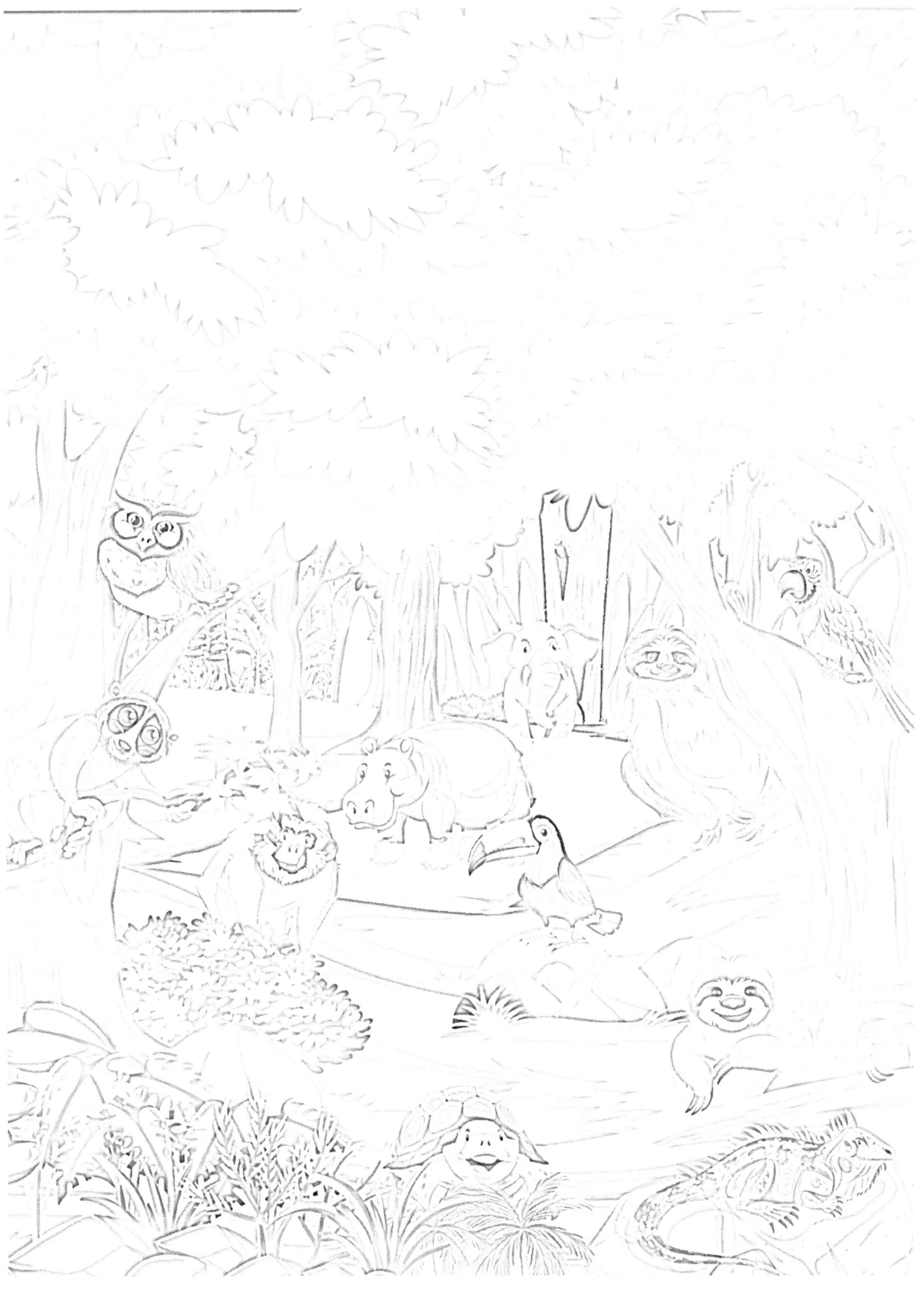

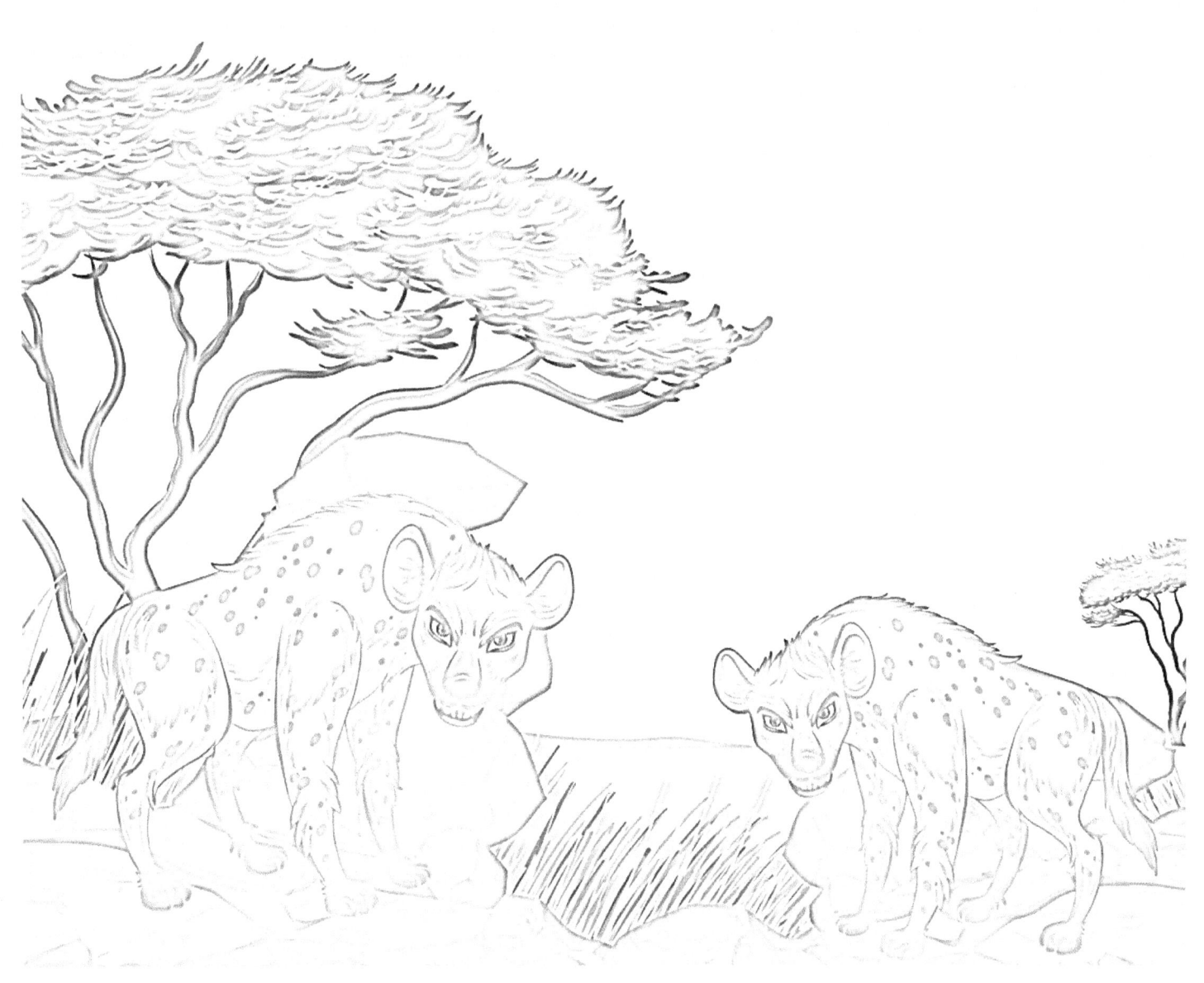

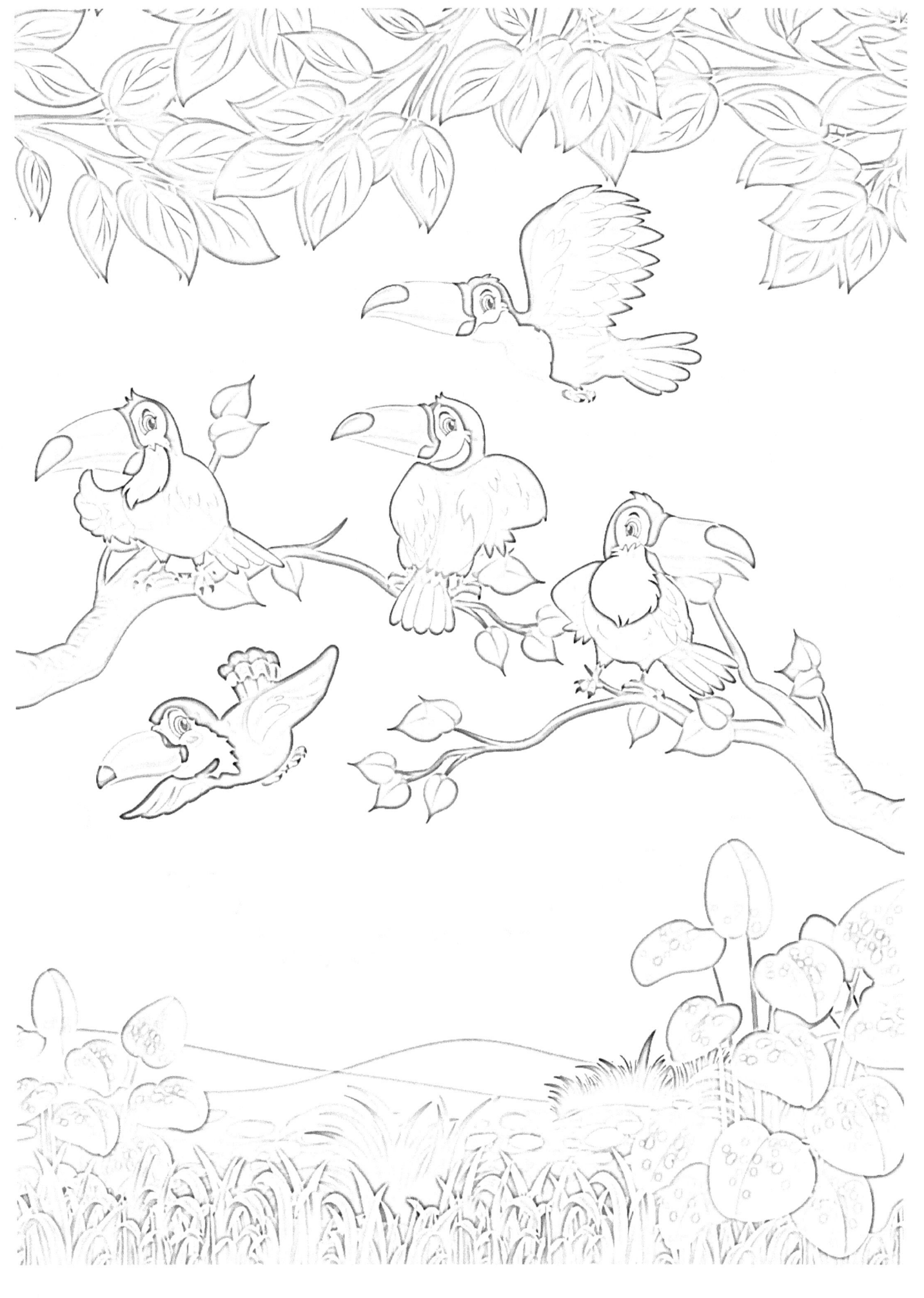

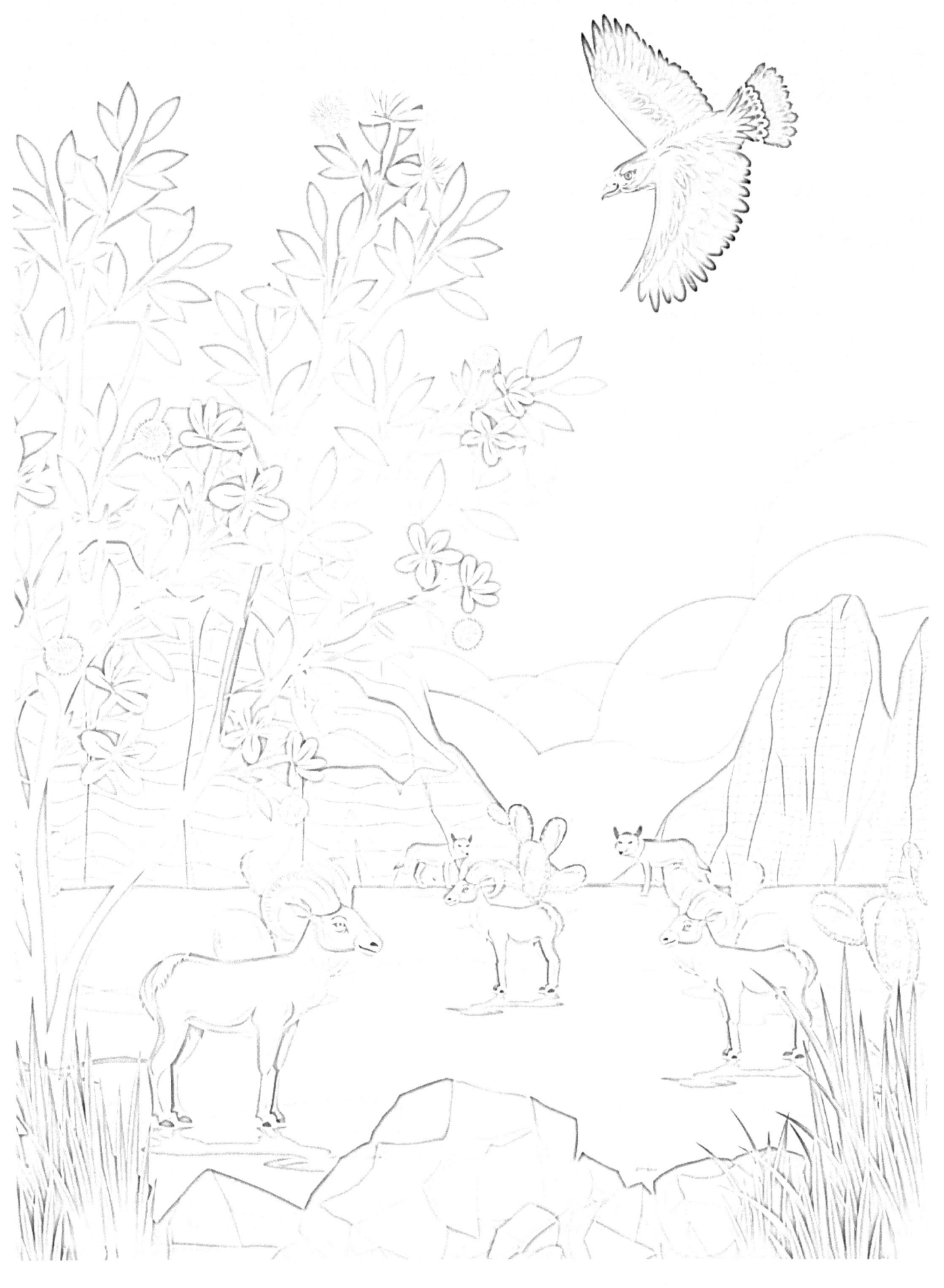

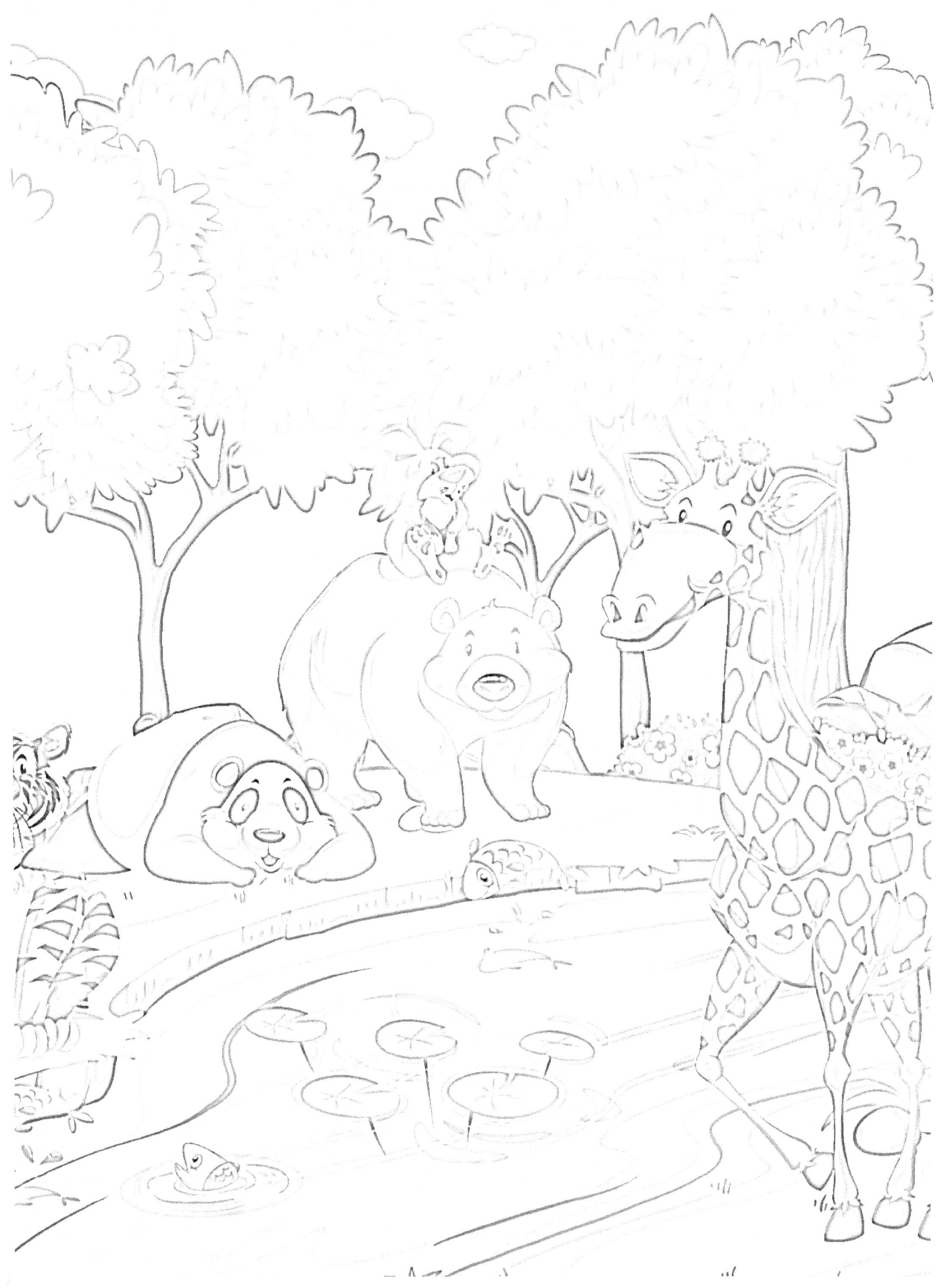

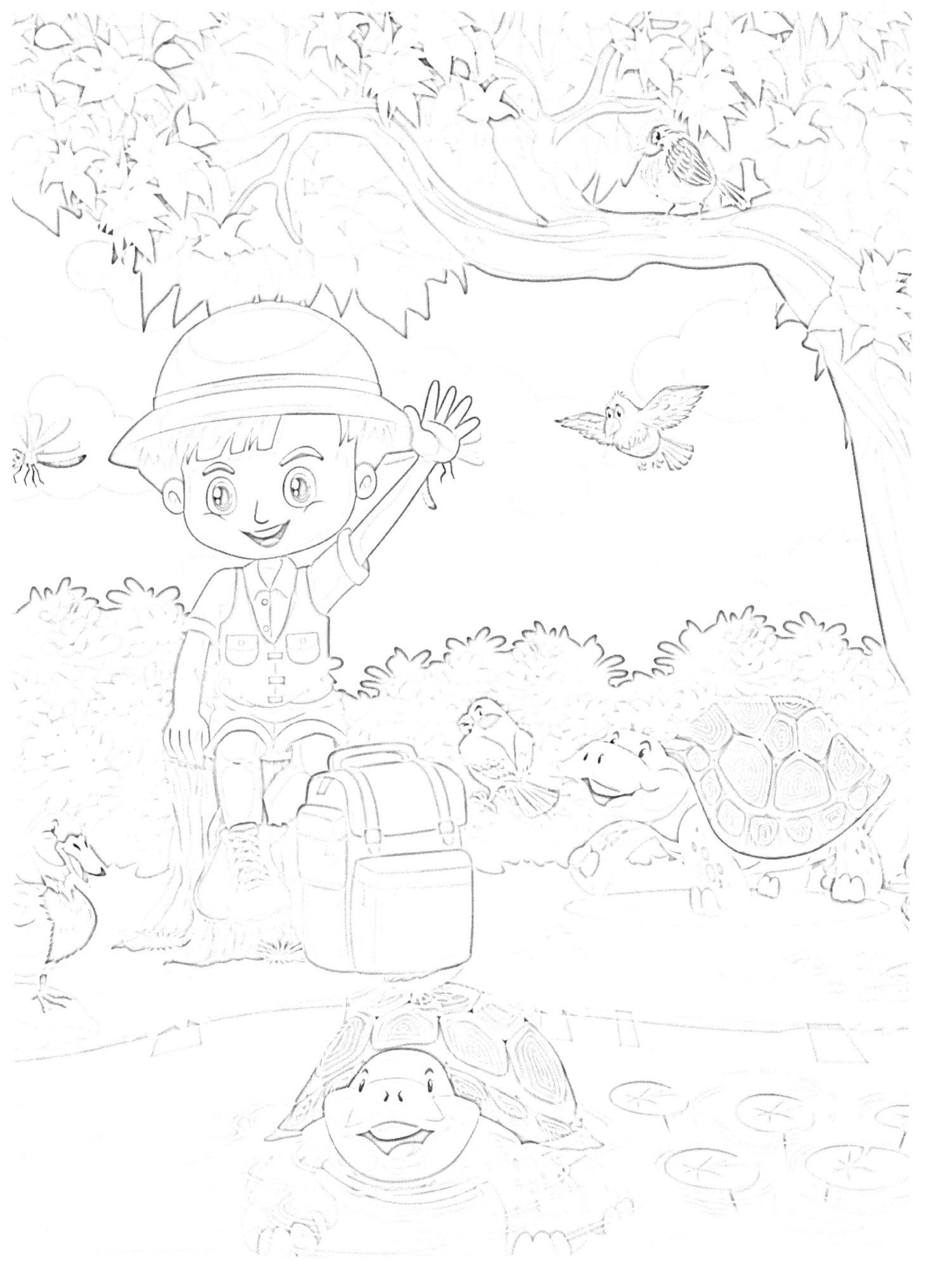

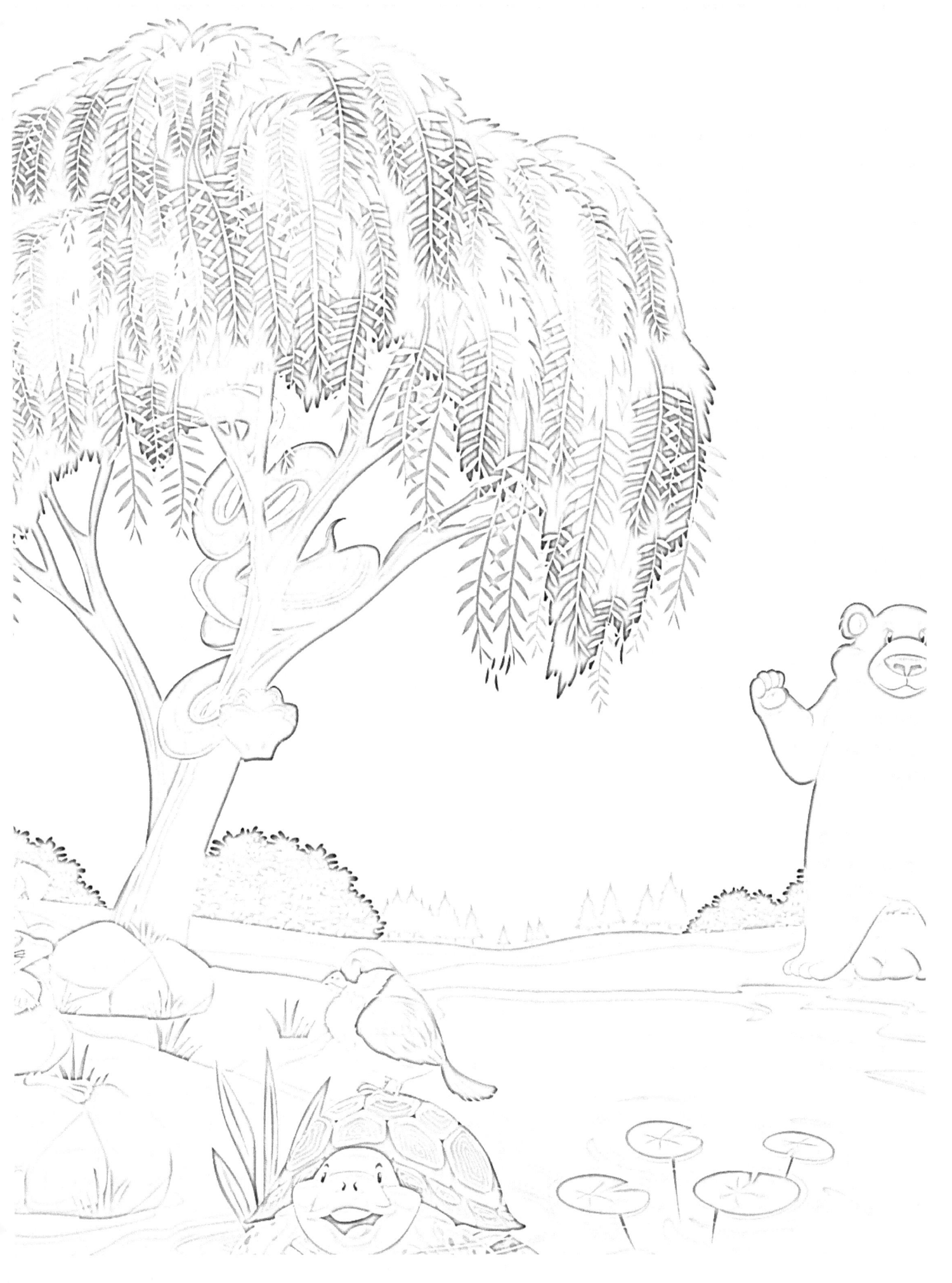

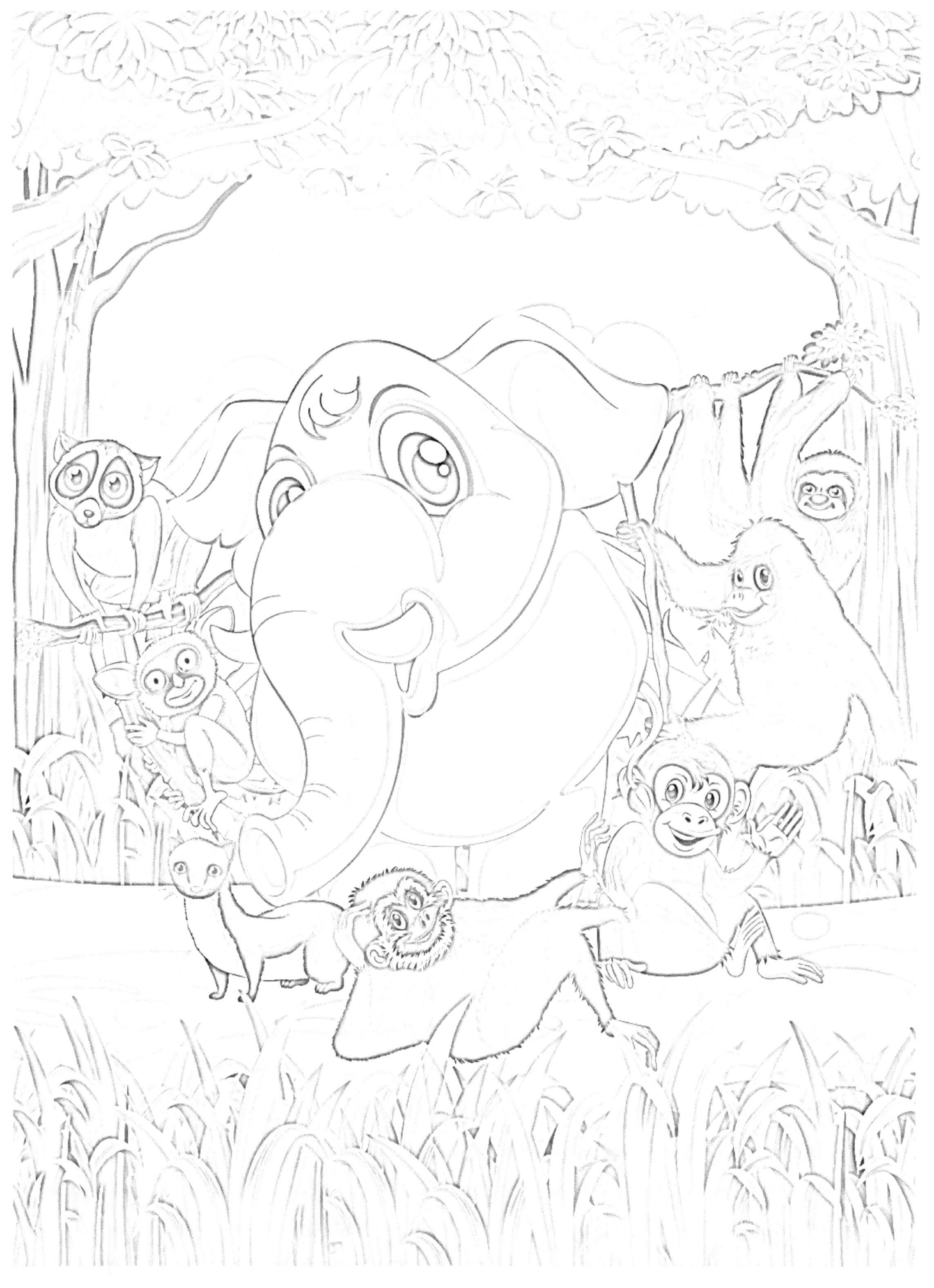

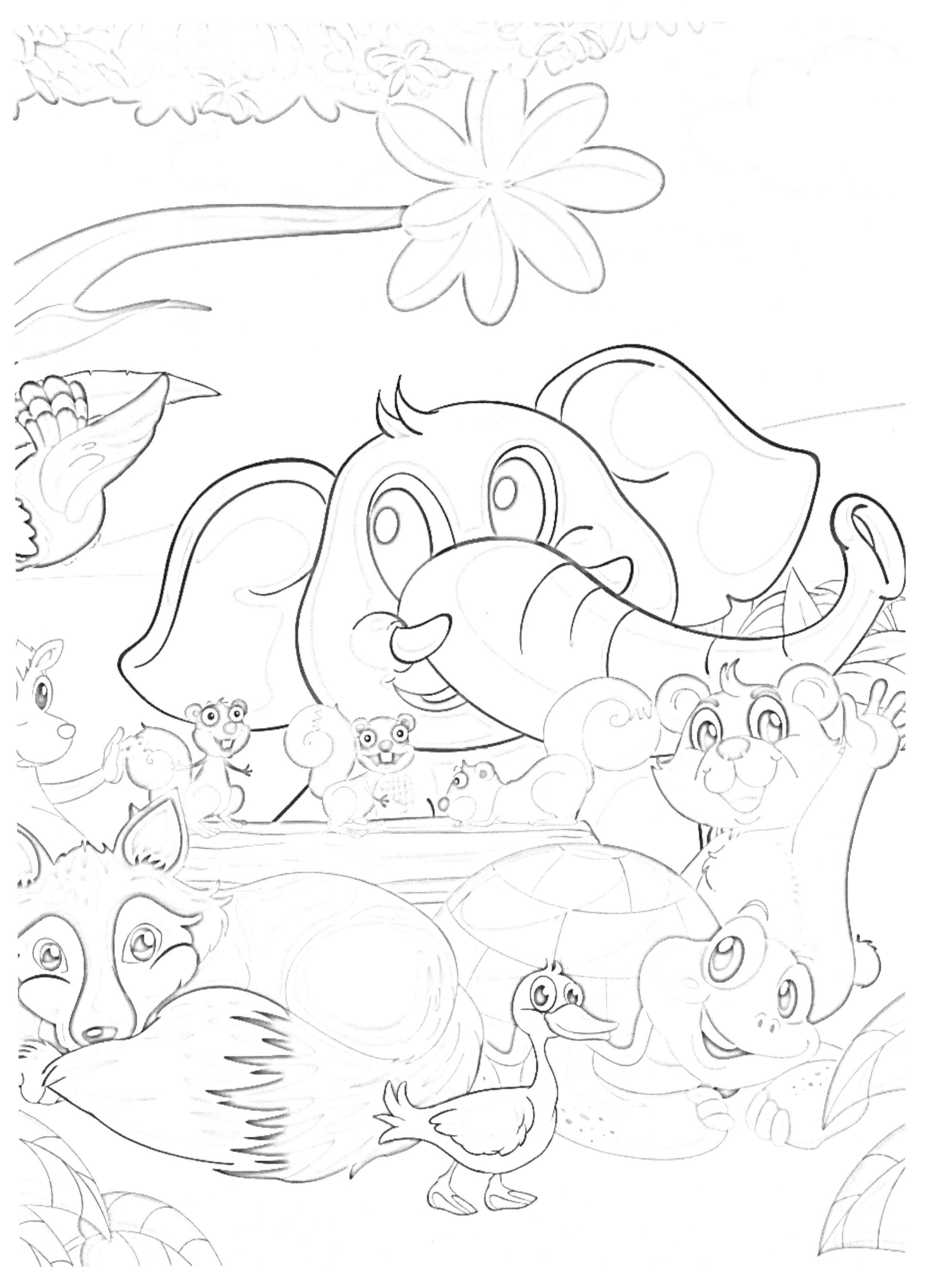